THE SOUND OF
HILO RAIN

THE SOUND OF HILO RAIN

ROY KODANI

WATERMARK
PUBLISHING

ISBN 978-1-935690-58-0

Library of Congress Control Number: 2014952939

Design and production
Mae Ariola

Cover photography
Hawai'i State Archives (front cover photo from
the Brother Bertram Collection)

Watermark Publishing
1000 Bishop St., Suite 806
Honolulu, HI 96813
www.bookshawaii.net
info@bookshawaii.net

Printed in the United States

To my daughters,
Regina Kodani and Candace Kodani Cheever,
with my warmest aloha
and deepest affection

CONTENTS

FOREWORD

On the eastern side of the Big Island of Hawai'i, the rain comes in tandem with the trade winds from the northeast and drenches the land from Kohala on the north to Ka'ū on the southern point of the island. In ancient Hawaiian culture, water is a symbol of growth, wealth and fertility. The complexity and the nuance of the word "fertility" have definitions of varying degrees of interpretations. The rain has different names depending on its gentleness or ferocity, and the season of the rainfall. The water from the highlands flows in rivers and streams to the sea, and it is the rain that makes the land verdant, lush, green and abundant with vegetation and flora. When the rain sweeps across the land, the sound of the rain is a symphony of music, light and soft, or thunderous and majestic in all its presence.

At night the sound of the gentle rain falling on the leaves of trees and on the palm fronds is *nahenahe* (sweet and soft), loving and romantic, stirring the heart and soothing the soul. In Hilo, the sound of the rain—like the two major rivers, Wailuku and Wailoa, that flow from the deep, unpopulated interior of the island into Hilo Bay—is the unconscious soul of Hilo. As the rain clouds fade into the darkness of the night, the *mahina poepoe* (full moon) rises from the eastern sky and the bluish brightness casts a spell as only a Hawaiian moon can, bringing forth *maluhia* (peace, quiet, serenity).

INTRODUCTION

The stories in this book are vignettes of people who lived on the Big Island of Hawai'i in the 1940s and '50s. Their common theme is the experience of growing up and coming of age in the small town of Hilo, when life was simple and the choices were few. Many of the modern conveniences either hadn't been invented yet, or just weren't part of life in Hilo. Although the Big Island's geographical features are certainly unique, the experiences in these stories are universal. Life in Hilo was influenced by the good and bad that exists everywhere, by natural disasters that profoundly changed its residents' lives, and inevitably by the luck of living in this particular place at this special time—and of being surrounded by people, specifically *nikkeijin* (Americans of Japanese ancestry) with sound values that shaped young people's lives forever.

ROMANCE AT THE SWIMMING HOLE

"Roy, after school you gotta go swimming with me at Orinoco," pleaded Asa, one of my best buddies.

The town of Hilo is located between two rivers: Wailoa and Wailuku. The rivers were like yin and yang. The Wailoa River is wide, placid and deep. Deep enough for boats to travel upstream for a mile or so. At the mouth of the river, commercial fishing boats called fishing sampans docked along the banks after being out to sea for three or four days, and the fish that were caught were sold at the auction house. During the late 1940s, there must have been about twenty or thirty commercial fishing boats. Now, there is only a handful. During those years, there was a thriving community, Waiākea Town, located alongside the river and facing Kamehameha Avenue, the main street in Hilo, which ran perpendicular to the river. The trains that used to run all the way from Honokaa, about fifty miles out of Hilo on the north, to Kapoho, about thirty miles south of Hilo, were housed, maintained and repaired at the roundhouse in Waiākea Town. The icehouse was also there. Ice to keep the fish fresh, the beer and soda drinks cold; ice for the icebox before refrigeration became a common thing; ice for shaved ice. Ice was an important part of our lives then. The old Japanese shipwrights built the fishing sampans, often times without any plans, merely from memory, on the waterfront. Waiākea Town is gone now, ravaged first in 1946 and ultimately destroyed by tidal waves in 1960. The sea nourishes us, feeds us, provides us with a livelihood, but the sea also destroys us. Eons ago, we came from the sea, and eons from now, could the sea take us all back again? Perhaps.

The other river on the north side of town, the Wailuku River, is different in all aspects from the Wailoa River, as night is different from day. The water runs fast and turbulently, even dangerously, especially after a heavy rainfall. There are huge boulders and lava outcroppings in the river. It goes far inland for miles and miles, and the source of the river lies deep in the rainforests far upland. One of the famous falls in the Hawaiian Islands is found on the river. Rainbow Falls, aptly named because the rays of the sun striking the mist of the falls creates a rainbow. Many of the streams flow into the Wailuku, and after a heavy rainstorm the river turns reddish brown from the silt of the soil that is washed into the river—soil from the fertile land that grew sugarcane, which was the main economy of the island in those days, but the sugar industry is now gone and acres of land which grew sugarcane lie farrow.

It was in the Wailuku River, a short walking distance from our elementary school, Hilo Union School, that there was an old swimming hole called Orinoco. We had to climb down, or more accurately, scamper down, a high, steep bank to get to a pool in the river. It was deep and greenish-black, very mysterious. This was Orinoco. It was like a river in a South American or African jungle, with tall trees and hanging vines. When you looked up the river, the growth was so thick; it was dark and forbidding. But, it was all this that added to the adventure of swimming at Orinoco. It wasn't until many years later that I was to learn that Orinoco was the name of a river in Brazil, but until then it was the only Orinoco that I knew.

"Why do you want to go swimming at Orinoco after school, Asa? There's lots of other things we can do," I said. "Besides, I didn't bring my swimming shorts."

"Just come with me," he pleaded again.

"And what about my swimming shorts? I'm not going to swim naked with all the people around, you know."

"Don't worry about it. I brought extra shorts for you."

"You're bigger than me. I hope it fits me. I don't want it to fall. How come this sudden interest in swimming?" I asked.

"I'll tell you on the way there. Hurry up after school, so we can go there as soon as possible. Don't waste time."

He didn't have to worry about that. I sure didn't hang around my classroom after school. Once the school bell rang, I made a mad dash out of class. I didn't care much for school then.

After school, Asa and I changed into our shorts, or rather into Asa's shorts, folded our pants and walked to Orinoco. We went down the muddy trail to the river holding on to the vines. Because Orinoco was popular, there was a whole bunch of boys and girls already there, some swimming, others sunbathing and others just lolling around. The boys looking at the girls, and the girls pretending not to notice the boys. I'm pretty sure they knew the boys were there.

"There she is, Roy. There she is," whispered Asa.

"Who?" I asked.

"There, by the big boulder," Asa said, pointing down the river. There were many girls in that direction and many of them were around big boulders.

"Which boulder? The river is full of boulders, Asa."

"Christ's sakes! The one in the white," he replied with disgust at my failure to see whomever he wanted me to see.

I looked at the girl wearing the white bathing suit. I probably stared at her. I was young and certainly lacked sophistication. I had not yet learned how to look at the opposite sex without staring. That would come years later, of course, with practice. She certainly wasn't someone from our school. Was she a student from the Catholic school? Or was she from Riverside School, which was located right across the street from our elementary school. To enroll in Riverside School, you had to take a special examination to qualify, a sort of elite school. It was an English standard school, where you spoke the Standard English and not pidgin English, a sort of Hawai'i patois.

"Who is she? She's not from our school, Asa?" I asked. It was like someone from Earth fraternizing with a woman from outer space. It was unheard of.

"Dummy, of course not. She's from Hilo Intermediate School."

"What! She's older than us."

Not only was she from outer space, she was an older woman, most likely an experienced older woman. God forbid! My good buddy, Asa, had gone off the deep end.

"So she's older. So what? What's the difference?" Really, when you think about it. What is the difference between being friendly with a younger woman or an older woman?

"Nothing, I guess. But, why someone older, Asa?"

"Roy, I love her."

Wow! Love. I had never heard anyone in real life, until then, express love for another person. In the movies, yes, but not in real life. Gee, this was serious stuff. I squinted to get a better look at her. She must be something for Asa to profess his love for her. Probably because she was older, maybe she was in the seventh grade. She did have a more mature look. One thing for sure, she filled out her bathing suit quite amply, I thought. She saw Asa and waved demurely. Not wildly like a sixth grader. Hey, this was something. I could see why Asa was smitten by this sophisticated young lady. She knew how to handle herself. Boy! No girl had ever waved to me demurely, for that matter. No girl had ever waved to me, period.

"Her name is Nancy," Asa said with a deep sigh.

"You mean you actually know her?" I asked incredulously.

"Of course. How else would I know her name? I met her a few weeks ago."

"Where?"

"Here at Orinoco, where else?"

"You met her here, and then what happened?"

"What do you mean, what happened?"

"I mean, what did you do?"

"What are you talking about, Roy?"

"Did you just go up to her and ask her name?"

"Be serious. You don't just go up to a girl and ask her name. Come on, you should know that."

"I don't know. That's why I'm asking you. How did you get to know her?"

"Gee. Do I have to teach you everything?"

"It would be nice. I may meet a girl too someday, Asa. I sure would like to know what to do and what to say."

"Just be casual, Roy. Just relax. Be cool. Don't tense up, Roy. Girls like guys who are suave."

"What is suave, Asa?"

"Ah, forget it, Roy. Do I have to teach you everything?"

"Sure would be nice, Asa."

"I think Nancy loves me, Roy."

Not only did Asa love Nancy, but Nancy loved Asa. This was romance. Just like the movies. In fact, this was better than the movies. This was really, really something. I was glad I had joined Asa at Orinoco. I was learning something. After this, everything else would be dull stuff.

"How do you know she loves you?" I asked.

"The way she looks at me, dummy."

"The way she looks at you?"

"Yeah, the way she looks at me."

"How does she look at you?"

"For Christ's sakes, do I have to tell you everything?"

"Sure would be nice, Asa."

"Well, she doesn't just look at me. Her eyes look deep into my eyes, you know what I mean?"

I truly didn't know what he meant. But, he continued, "She looks at me like she's trying to talk to me with her eyes, not only her mouth, if you know what I mean?"

"No, I don't know what you mean."

"Oh, forget it. Let's go over and talk to her."

"What do you talk to an older girl about, Asa. I don't know what to say." I could tell I was trying his patience, but Asa was a real buddy of mine. He was very patient and understanding. You know how you get along very well with some people? Asa and I were like that. Good buddies.

"Just talk about anything. Anything that comes to your head. Just be natural. But, for crying out loud, don't act like a kid, Roy."

"Don't sweat it, Asa. People tell me I'm mature for my age. I'm eleven, eleven and a half to be exact."

"OK, just don't act stupid, that's all."

Nancy was lying against a boulder, facing the sun. She was tall and her hips were full. My throat suddenly went dry. I had an urge to drink water. Here I was in the middle of the river with water flowing around us, but there was no water to drink. Life sometimes is so ironic.

With her hands folded in the back of her head, she smiled and said, "Hi, Asa. I was hoping you would come today. I'm glad you came. Who's your friend?"

"That's Roy. He doesn't know too many older girls, so he's shy."

Oh my god! I wished he hadn't said that. I was nervous before, but now I was devastated. How could I act cool?

Nancy said, "Hi, Roy. You don't have to be shy. He's cute, Asa."

She called me cute. Cute. I didn't like being cute. Cute reminded me of a puppy or a fluffy white rabbit. They were cute, not me.

"He's all right. We've been good friends for a long time," said Asa.

"He's got skinny legs, though."

I looked down at my legs. I always thought my legs were average, not necessarily skinny. She certainly made me feel inadequate. I didn't like being criticized by a stranger, even if she was an older person.

"What school do you go to, Roy?" she asked.

"Hilo Union," I answered.

"You mean Hilo Onion, don't you?" she said teasingly.

If she were a boy, I would have punched her right in the mouth. I didn't like her making fun of my school.

She climbed to the top of the boulder and sat with her arms wrapped around her legs. Looking down, she smilingly asked, "Roy, have you kissed a girl?"

How was I to respond to a question like that? Boys my age didn't go around kissing girls, at least not on the lips, we didn't. Not even on the cheeks, for that matter.

I looked up at her and said in a steady and in as manly voice as I could, "That's none of your business."

"Ha! I bet you never kissed a girl."

I looked at Asa for help. She was persistent. Asa stood there with his arms folded, looking gaga at her. What a big help he was.

If ever there was a time to tell a white lie, this was it. "Sure, I kissed a girl," I replied as nonchalantly as I could.

"What's her name?"

"Why should I tell you? You wouldn't know her anyway."

"Maybe I do. Tell me, Roy."

"She lives in the country," I said. Boy, my white lies were getting blacker each time I opened my mouth. This girl was leading me down the road to moral decay and doom. My father had warned me never to tell a lie. *"Roy, one lie leads to another. Pretty soon, you tell so many lies, the lies catch up with you. You won't know which way is up and which way is down. Honesty is the best policy. The best thing is never start telling even one white lie."*

She shot back with another question. "Where in the country?"

She was relentless.

I could not stop now. My manhood was at stake. "In Kona." Kona was on the other side of the island and in those days it took about three to four hours by car to get to the town of Kailua, the main town in Kona, and even today it takes a good two hours from Hilo to Kailua. When I was in elementary school, if you went to Kona, you stayed there overnight because it was such a long and tedious trip. Certainly, she wouldn't know anyone in Kona, I thought.

"Kona? I have uncles and aunties and cousins in Kona. Maybe you kissed one of my cousins? Tell me her name. It could be one of them, Roy."

She had me cornered like a rat. Nancy was like a patient, smooth cat ready at the draw to spring the trap. I had to think fast. My brain went into high gear. I couldn't let her pounce upon me now. I squirmed around and shuffled my feet. I cleared my voice and said, "I promised her I would never, never tell anyone I kissed her. A promise is a promise and I'm not going to break my promise," I answered triumphantly.

"I still think you never kissed a girl."

"Why don't you believe me? You believe me, huh, Asa?" I asked.

"Sure, Kodani, I believe you," he answered hesitantly as though not quite convinced. Asa was a real friend. Friends believed friends.

I could see why Asa fell for Nancy. She had big eyes and when she smiled, the joints in my knees felt like rubber. Her skin was tan, the color of maple syrup that I poured over my pancakes.

"Hey, I going to swim," I said, and turned and stomped off.

"Is something bothering your friend?" I could hear Nancy ask Asa.

"Nah, he's never been around girls much, that's all."

After the swim, as we were walking home, I asked Asa, "How does it feel to be in love?"

"Why do you want to know?"

"I wanna know, that's all."

"For one thing, you can't think about anything else except for the girl you love."

"You mean more than baseball and sports and things like that?"

"Yeah, she's on my mind all the time. I can't wait for after school to come around so I can rush off to Orinoco to see her. And, when I get there, you know, sometimes, we don't even say a word to each other, but I feel really good just to be with her."

"How do you know that she's the one for you? I mean, there's a lot of other girls?"

"Gee, you really wanna know, huh, Kodani?"

"I wanna know because someday I may fall in love too."

"You will know when that happens."

"How?"

"You will see her and she will see you, and both of you will know. She will be special in your eyes and you will be special in her eyes. Your heart will pound away and you will feel weak. Inside you will feel warm and you will want to be gentle to her and to protect her. Others will tell you she's too tall, or she's too heavy, or she goes to another church or she's another nationality. Oh, people will tell you all kinds of things about her to try to convince you that she's not right for you. They will tell you that it's for your own good. But, whatever others tell you, this feeling for the girl will be so strong that nothing can tear you away from her. She will be so special you will think about her all the time and you will try to think about all the ways to make her happy. When you have this kind of feeling for a girl, I think it's called love."

I was impressed by his explanation of love. What could I say to him after that?

Asa's romance with Nancy grew hot and heavy. Asa would just look at her and he would break into a wide smile. Nancy would dive into the dark pool in her stunning white bathing suit, and he would dive after her. She would shriek and he would laugh. I would stand by the boulders and watch them. I felt like an intruder. After a while, he would not even ask me to join him. I presumed he was meeting Nancy. I did not see him for two or three weeks, but I did not think much about it, for that matter. He and I were in different classes, and I thought our paths were not crossing. I concluded that he was spending more of his time with Nancy.

Asa deserved his experience with love because of a tragedy that befell him shortly after, before the end of the school year.

One day after school, as I was sitting with a bunch of guys talking story under the cool shade of the old ironwood tree that used to stand on the grounds of the school facing the Catholic church, Asa walked by and said with a big, warm smile, "Hey, Kodani, I won't be seeing you again."

"How come? You getting married?" I said. All the guys rolled on the ground laughing their heads off.

"Nah, I'm dying." He answered so casually, so flippantly that I assumed he was joking.

"What do you mean, Asa? Nobody young dies."

"Not in my case. My doctor says that I don't have much time to live. I'm going to the hospital tomorrow morning for surgery and I may not make it."

I still didn't know whether he was joking or telling the truth. I stuttered, "But, you don't even look sick. In fact, you look the same. Your usual self, Asa."

"I don't look sick but I've got a problem in my brain."

Ordinarily, I would have told him he always had a problem with his brain, but it was not a reason for him to die. But, I knew this was not a joking matter. The other guys were quiet too. I asked him, "What's wrong?"

"I was having really bad headaches, and so I went to the doctor. My doctor wasn't too sure, so he sent me to a specialist in Honolulu. That's why you haven't seen me for a while, Kodani. I was in Honolulu. I bet you thought I had forgotten you, eh, Kodani?"

"Aren't you scared?"

"At first, I was. I didn't want to die. I used to have bad dreams too, just thinking about dying, I guess. After a while, I figured things out. I think there must be a reason for all this. I don't think things just happen. If I should die, I'm pretty sure there was a good reason for me dying so young. I don't wanna think about dying. It's so depressing. It seems like I'm not going to have fun again. Hey, Kodani, we had some good times, huh?"

I remember I stood as he walked away. What do you do when you're eleven years old and your good buddy tells you he is dying? I didn't know what else to say or what to do. He was one of my best friends. He would visit me at my home and I would visit him at his home. He would eat with us and I would eat with him and his family. He was bigger than I and when we wrestled, he would naturally always win. We had a lot of fun together, and we would laugh at all the crazy things we said. We would quarrel about insignificant things but we always remained steadfast friends, even when he was spending time with Nancy at Orinoco.

We were in the Boy Scouts together, and after the meetings, we would go to the store and buy candy. We would walk down Waianuenue Avenue and when we reached Kapiolani Street, I would turn right and head home, about a five-minute walk. Asa had another thirty minutes to walk to his home in Pueo. I used to wonder what he thought about while walking home alone.

The thought of Asa dying did not quite register. It was very hard for me to accept it. We were both young and we had many, many more years ahead of us. We were just kids. Life was just starting for us. To me, then, death was for the elderly, not for someone young and robust like Asa.

"Hey, good luck, Asa," I said. That's all I could say.

"Yeah, thanks, Kodani." I can still see Asa walking alone toward town. He was wearing a blue jacket, a blue sports shirt and khaki trousers, swinging his arms as though he was headed toward the river to Orinoco. He never looked back. I know that if he had, and called out for me, I would have ran and joined him. Maybe, he preferred to be alone. I don't know how he was able to face the bleak uncertainty so optimistically.

Asa didn't make it. He died after surgery. He went into the hospital in Honolulu to prepare for the surgery. I learned later from my mother that all the nurses fell in love with him. He was such a happy guy, full of fun, always looking at the bright side of things. He knew that his chance of surviving was slim, but he never gave up hope. To the end, he was cheerful. Asa's mother told my mother that the evening before surgery, Asa told his family, "Don't be sad, if I should die. God is calling me home, that's all."

My family and I went to his funeral. One of the first funerals I attended. I was so sad, but somehow I couldn't cry. It didn't seem fitting to cry. Asa wouldn't have wanted me to cry. With all the fun we had, he would have said, "Hey, Kodani, why are you crying for? Don't act stupid."

Oh, yes, one final thing. Nancy was there at his funeral. She wore a white dress, the same color as her bathing suit. She cried her heart out. I think everyone in the church could hear her sobbing loudly and uncontrollably. I'm glad she could make it. Asa loved her so much. For a brief moment in his life, she meant so much to him. She was every-thing to him.

After Asa died, I never went back to Orinoco ever again. All my friends used to invite me to join them, but the memories of the good times with Asa and Nancy still remain with me. Swimming in the cool waters on a hot day would have been refreshing, but I just couldn't go back. I couldn't. ◖

A LONG-LOST FRIEND

As an attorney working long hours, six days and often seven days a week, constantly talking to people, being in a pressure cooker environment, I seek to recharge my energy periodically by escaping to solitude. To peace and quiet. By being alone, I can contemplate and think things out and clear the cobwebs. I return refreshed. This is a temporary respite from the hard charging and relentless aggressiveness of my profession. I do not seek serenity by living alone permanently. I would think such a life would be lonely. We all need companionship, friendship, a relationship with other human beings. This is a simple story of a friendship.

My father sold fertilizer in his hardware store, and among his best customers were farmers. There were farmers with large tracts of land with sophisticated equipment and machinery, and there were truck farmers attempting to eke out a living from small parcels of land. I can still remember farmers who tilled the soil laboriously with a mule and a plow. Sometimes, my father would deliver fertilizer, farm supplies and tools to farmers who were unable to come to the store to pick up their purchases. One of them was an elderly Korean immigrant, Mr. Choy, who lived in the cool uplands above Hilo in an area called Kaumana. Mr. Choy lived alone and rarely, if ever, came to town.

There were only a handful of people of Korean ancestry living in Hilo when I was growing up. Although the congregation of the Korean Christian Church was few in number, they were very active church members. The Korean community was supportive of each other. The commonality of language and culture is a strong bond among immigrants of the same ancestry or nationality. The fewer people from the old country, the closer the community.

My father did not speak nor understand Korean, and Mr. Choy did not speak nor understand English too well. Yet, somehow, Mr. Choy and my father were able to communicate with each other.

My father would greet Mr. Choy, "Hello, Choy-san. How are you today?"

Mr. Choy would respond, "Hello, Bonemeal-san."

In those days, it was socially acceptable to call someone by his occupation rather than by his name. Such as milkman-san, fishman-san, postman-san. People referred to my father as bonemeal-san because bonemeal was a type of plant food. I guess he could just as well have been called fertilizer-san.

My father would continue, "I bring three bags of fertilizer to make cabbage grow and two bags to make carrots grow. OK?"

"OK, Bonemeal-san. I no can pay this week. I pay next time when the cabbage big. OK?"

"OK, Choy-san. I write in my book." My father had a black composition book in which he would note the name of the customer, date of sale, merchandise sold and the amount owed. When the customer paid, he marked a large "PAID" across the notation and the date paid. It was a simple bookkeeping system, and as far as I can remember no one ever questioned any of my father's entry.

After the business was concluded, Mr. Choy would enter the shack in which he lived and return with three bottles of soda pop. One for my dad, one for himself and one for me. Because he didn't have a refrigerator or an icebox, the soda pop was warm, but my father would drink it with great relish as though it was the most delicious soda in the whole wide world. To show how much he enjoyed it, my father would smack his lips and say, "The soda taste good because the air here is good."

Mr. Choy would break into a wide smile and nod his head in agreement. He certainly appreciated my father's compliments.

I once asked my father after we had left Mr. Choy's, "Dad, the soda was really warm. It didn't taste good. I could hardly take a sip because it was so warm. Did you really enjoy drinking it?"

"I agree warm soda is not as enjoyable to drink as cold soda. But, you must remember, Mr. Choy knew we were coming to deliver the fertilizer and he walked all the way to the grocery store a mile away and carried the bottles of soda all the way back. He did that because he is a very kind and thoughtful man. His home may not be a mansion, but Mr. Choy wants to extend his hospitality to us. He may be rough, but he is a gracious man. When I think what he had to go through to make us feel welcome, Mr. Choy's warm soda tastes better than the coldest soda served on a hot day by people who are not sincere."

One more thing about Mr. Choy and his serving soda pop to us. Usually, when people served soda to me, they would ask, "Roy, what kind of soda would you like?" My favorite then was either orange or lime, and I would answer, "Do you have orange, please?" At least, I was offered a choice. With Mr. Choy, he would serve me whatever he had available. Once he offered me a strawberry soda, and I disliked strawberry soda. Warm strawberry soda was even worse. Ordinarily, I would have put up a fuss, but I had remembered what my father had told me about Mr. Choy going out of his way to pick up the bottles of soda pop, and so, I drank it although I certainly did not enjoy drinking it.

My father and Mr. Choy would chat for a good five to ten minutes under the shade of a milo tree. They would talk about vegetables, insects that marauded the plants, the price of vegetables, the hardship endured by farmers and whatever else that came to their minds.

As they talked story, I would wander around the farm full of curiosity. I enjoyed running through the tall green grass growing in a patch on his farm. I don't know why I enjoyed running back and forth through the tall grass. I once peeked into Mr. Choy's shack. He had no electricity, only a kerosene stove and a Coleman lamp hanging from the low ceiling. He had no running water, only a large mayonnaise gallon jar with water. He had no bed, only an old mattress laid on a wooden platform made from lumber that others had dumped in a trash pile somewhere. It was then that I learned it really does not require much for us to live in this world, if we can be satisfied with what we have. When I think about it, we really don't need much to live. It is not necessary to live in a big, fancy house or to own many luxury accessories.

I remember distinctly one conversation he had with my father. He was describing the poverty in Korea and why he came to Hawai'i. "My family in Korea very poor. Rich farmer hire my father, brothers and me to work in rice fields. We pull the plow from early in the morning to late at night. The rich farmer water buffalo sit in the shade and chew grass. Buffalo, no work. Cheaper for rich farmer to hire us than feed water buffalo. If water buffalo work, must feed water buffalo. I work hard. Life for poor man in Korea very hard."

After a while, my father would say, "Let's be going, Roy. Say thank you to Mr. Choy for the soda." I would and Mr. Choy would bow like an Asian gentleman. I can still see Mr. Choy in his tattered straw hat, denim shirt and khaki trousers, waving to us as we rode down the bumpy dirt lane to the main road. He would crane his neck as we turned the corner and drove out of sight. Young as I was, I thought how lonely he must be to live alone so far away from others in the uplands of Kaumana.

As the years went by and Mr. Choy got older, he purchased less and less fertilizer, and finally, he stopped ordering fertilizer. My father lost track of him, and I certainly forgot about Mr. Choy. Whenever we were in the Kaumana neighborhood visiting a family friend of ours, I would think of Mr. Choy momentarily and wonder what had happened to him.

"Daddy, where do you think Mr. Choy is?"

"I don't know. I know he didn't have a family. I don't think he had any relatives in Hawai'i. I don't think he went back to Korea because, as he said, life in the old country is harder than life in America. That's the reason most people came to America. Because, no matter how bad it is, life here is much, much better than the old country."

Gradually, I forgot about Mr. Choy and I think my father did also. We were all caught up in our own activities that it was easy to forget our friends and people we had known. One night my father's church social club visited the old folks' home to entertain the patients there. In those days, the geriatric care home was in fact referred to as the old folks' home. The term "senior citizens" was to come years later. It was funded by the State of Hawai'i and the patients were indigents. Although the main purpose was to entertain the patients, there was another reason to visit the patients. It was to express appreciation to the older immigrants who had sacrificed so much so that the younger generations could have a better life than they did.

My father wrote a skit referred to as *shibai* about the sacrifices made by the first-generation immigrants. He assembled a group of his friends to perform the shibai, and they rehearsed several times a week so that the drama became more realistic as time went on. As the day got closer for the shibai, my father got excited. He was sure that it would be a success and that the patients would appreciate a shibai depicting all the hardship and sorrows they had endured as immigrants.

As I learned later, the patients thoroughly enjoyed the skit. Some of them even cried as they relived their early days in Hawai'i. And, on the same night, my father experienced a very emotional and unforgettable encounter.

When he came home, he raced up the front steps shouting, "Guess who I saw tonight at the old folks' home?"

I wouldn't have known where to start. At my age, I didn't know too many older folks, much less old folks at the home.

My mother asked, "Is there someone there we know, Daddy? I don't think I know anyone there. If there is, it's a complete surprise to me."

"Yes, there is someone we know, Mama. There really is."

"Well, please tell us. Don't keep us in suspense. I cannot even guess who it can be."

"When I tell you who it is, you are going to be surprised. I know you will be."

"I wish you would tell us instead of dangling this mystery before us."

"It's Mr. Choy."

My mother couldn't remember and so she asked, "Who is Mr. Choy?"

"You know, Mr. Choy, the farmer, who lived alone in Kaumana. I used to deliver fertilizer to him."

"Oh, yes, now I remember. It's been so long I had forgotten about him."

"Well, Mama, I had forgotten about him too. We put on the shibai and everybody enjoyed it. They laughed at the funny parts and they cried at the sad parts. After the play was over, some of the patients came over to say it was good that people remembered the old days in order to appreciate what we have now. They said we should not forget what the old folks did. It was still early, and so I walked around to say hello to the patients in the wheelchairs. Since I don't know anybody there, I shook people's hands and made small talk. There was a skinny, old man hunched over in his wheelchair sitting alone in the back of the room. No one was talking to him, and I thought I should go over and say something to him. After all, we were there to cheer the old folks up. When I approached him, the old man grabbed my hand. He said, 'Thank you, thank you. You come see me.'

"At first, I thought the old man was senile. Then, I thought he was just glad to have us perform the shibai for them. But, he held onto my hands very tightly and said, 'Bonemeal-san, thank you. You come see me. Nobody come see me. Many people here have friends who come see them. Me, I have nobody. Nobody. Nobody come see me. But, I tell everybody here I have friend. My friend someday come see me. Nobody believe me. They think I have no friend. Now, they see me talk to you. Now, they know I have friend.'

"The old man was Mr. Choy. Tears flowed down his cheek. He was so happy to see me. Let me tell you this. When I saw his tears, I choked up. He began crying. Everybody looked at us. He just held my hands tightly. He wouldn't let go. He wanted so much to tell me what had happened to him. 'Me live here long, long time. I wanna go home, Kaumana. But me now old. Nurse tell me I need somebody take care me. I say OK. But, nurse not my friend. Only take care me. Me no friend here.' I asked him, 'Choy-san, they take good care of you here?' 'Oh, yes, Bonemeal-san, plenty good care. They give me everything me need. Everything very, very good. But, me have no friend. Your boy big now? He run in the grass near my house. I nevah cut the grass. Your boy always run in the grass. He was happy, yeah.' 'Yeah, Mr. Choy, he was happy to run around in the tall grass.'

"Finally, when it was time to leave, he cried out, 'Bonemeal-san, no go, no go. You stay some more. Nobody talk to me. Me, no friend. You, my friend.' I stood up and said out loud so that everyone could hear, 'Choy-san, you my long-time friend from Kaumana. You number one farmer in Kaumana. Nobody forget you in Kaumana. No worry, Choy-san, now I know where you live. I come visit you again.' He cried and cried and wouldn't let go of my hands. Finally, one of the nurses came over and said to him, 'Mr. Choy, don't worry your friend will come and visit you again. Won't you?' I said, 'Yes, don't worry, I will come the first chance I have.' Then, he released my hands. As I was leaving, he waved to me like he used to in Kaumana."

My mother said, "It all goes to show that just as important as food and water and the air we breathe, we all need someone to talk to. A husband, a wife, a companion, a friend. A person to share with, the good as well as the bad. The human heart requires love and affection and understanding to survive."

"You right, Mama. When you come to it, it is not money or wealth that brings happiness. It is friendship. We are blessed and must be thankful if we can measure our wealth in the number of friends we have. I guess this is what life is about. We are all born into this world to be brothers and sisters to one another. No matter who we are or what we do, basically, the one thing we can share without too much sacrifice is a little of ourselves. To extend our hand of friendship. It doesn't cost too much and it doesn't require too much."

In the spring of 1990, my father and I were in Kaumana visiting friends. We happened to ride by the property that used to be Mr. Choy's farm. Only one supporting post of the shack remained and the land was covered with weeds and brush. The milo tree where my father and Mr. Choy used to chat in the shade was still standing, but it did not look the same. It looked somewhat tattered with less leaves and it did not look as tall as I remembered it. We got out of the car and from the side of the road we stood and looked at the land in silence. But what I saw and what I think my father saw was not the land as it currently is but a farm and a good, gracious man long gone. The unforgettable memories of the tall, green grass of summer, swept by the cool breeze of the Kaumana highlands, and of me holding a strawberry soda pop bottle with my two small hands came flooding back. Suddenly, I was gripped with melancholy. ♦

ELEVATORS AND ESCALATORS IN HILO

Thee quaintness of Hilo lies in the fact that its soul remains tied to the 1940s and 1950s, even with the coming of the large Mainland stores. In the years to come, it may very well be the quaintness that will attract *malihini* (outsiders) and foreigners to this quiet and relatively safe town that may regretfully change Hilo forever.

The notion that Hilo has not substantially changed is supported by the number of elevators and escalators on the east side of Hawai'i Island.

Many years ago one of my aunts living in Hilo had to go to the third floor of the Federal Building. At that time the Third Circuit Court was on the third floor, and she had to get a copy of a legal document. I must have been about ten or eleven years old at that time.

"Roy, I have to go to da numba tree floor of da Federal Building. You can come wit' me, huh?"

"Sure. You want me to help you with something?"

"No. No need do anyting. You just come wit' me."

I thought maybe she wanted me to talk to someone at the court, because many older *nisei* (second-generation) men and women spoke only pidgin English and they were hesitant when speaking to people in authority.

On the day of appearing at the court, my aunt and I approached the elevator, which was the only elevator in Hilo at that time. My aunt then confessed to me in a hushed tone of voice, "Roy, dis is da first time I'm going to use da elevata, and you go help me get to the numba tree floor. OK?"

Well, it was also my first time using the elevator, because until then I had no reason to go to the court located on the third floor.

We both got into the elevator, and I looked around. My aunt, meanwhile, was perspiring. She said, "Oh, dis ting really small, yeah? I no can stand small places."

There were three buttons: 1, 2 and 3. I pressed 3, and the elevator began moving. *Wow!* I thought, *that wasn't too hard.* For my first elevator ride, I was making great progress in operating it. My aunt's next comment was, "Ho, dis ting moving fast, yeah?" At that time I didn't know if it was moving fast or slow because I had no other elevator experience to compare it with. I just stood there marveling at the movement of the elevator.

When it finally stopped on the third floor, my aunt remarked, "Was not too bad, yeah, Roy?"

Now and then, when I get into an elevator, I recall my first elevator ride in Hilo. It is the first of this or the first of that that you always remember.

Today there are about 139 commercial elevators on the Big Island, according to Bert Yorita, branch manager of Mitsubishi Elevator & Escalator Company. It is not a large number.

There are even fewer escalators in East Hawai'i. Yorita informed me that escalators are counted separately, that is, one for the escalator that goes down and another for the escalator that does up. In East Hawai'i, there are only six escalators.

Do you know where some of them are?

Answer: At the Hilo Airport.

Progress in Hilo may not necessarily be gauged by the traffic lights on the public roads. It may be the number of elevators and escalators. ◆

CAMPING UNDER THE OLD AVOCADO TREE

The darkness that follows the close of day has a way of transforming the bravest of boys into—let's be honest—into cowards, particularly if a cemetery is no more than two football fields away. The gloom of night plays games with our minds and gradually fear builds up to a climatic crescendo that our minds cross the line from rationality to a breaking point that thereafter no matter what is said to persuade us otherwise, our imagination runs wild at each strange sight seen and eerie sound heard lurking around us. Amazingly, an object seen during the day is not the same when seen at night. It usually appears larger, more threatening, scarier at night. Moonlight is no help. It may even make it worse. Shadows cast by the moonlight adds another forbidding dimension to the object. Take, for instance, a dead tree trunk. During the day, you may not even notice an ordinary tree trunk alongside the road, but that same tree trunk at night will appear to you like a squat, headless monster with outstretched scrawny arms waiting to pounce upon you as you walk by.

As we hunched in our Army surplus pup tent, whispering to each other, we peered into the darkness hoping to catch a glimpse of the mysterious "thing" that threw a diabolical dancing shadow upon our tent, a shadow that seem to tower over us. When the night wind cut sharply across the bushes, the shadow pranced eerily and moaned hauntingly a dirge of sadness. Darkness, or the dread of darkness, can drive boys into mass hysteria of fear and panic.

Before darkness had descended, we had prepared a typical Hawai'i campfire dinner. The rice tasted like buckshot but, then again, no one is perfect. The fried Spam and eggs weren't too bad. For some reason, which is still unknown to me, Spam has always been standard fare in Hawai'i. You can always tell a true son or daughter of Hawai'i. He or she can prepare Spam a hundred different ways. Fried, baked, diced, with vegetables, as sandwiches, with soy sauce, with Chinese oyster sauce, in omelets, with noodles (hot or cold) and so forth and so on. Canned corn was heated in open cans, hobo style. Dinner wasn't fancy but we had lots to eat and we thoroughly enjoyed our dinner. When I think about it now, it was not the meal that was so enjoyable. It was the fact that we had prepared dinner ourselves, not our mothers. There was no one to tell us what to do and what not to do. It was being outdoors on a clear summer night with the full July moon hanging low and not a care in the world.

We all did our share to prepare dinner, the seven of us boys who lived in the neighborhood. No one was in charge; no one supervised. We all knew what to do and we did it.

"Let's tell ghost stories after we eat," suggested Andy.

"Yeah, let's tell ghost stories. The spookier the better," we all chimed in. It's easy to be brave at twilight, when you can still see everything around you.

"Did you guys hear the one about the white ghost dog?" asked Corky. "It's a real hair raiser. When I heard it, I got cold chills, even if it was a hot, summer day. It's about this dog looking for his dead master. I gotta tell you guys when it gets darker. It's no fun telling a ghost story in daylight. I'll wait until it gets pitch black."

Tommy said, "I know one about this old lady with white hair wearing a white dress without any feet who comes floating around. That's a story that should make your hair stand. At least, it made mine stand."

"You guys know about the ghost who comes out in the cemetery, huh?" asked Bobby.

"What ghost?" we all asked.

"People say that one of the people buried there is a soldier," replied Bobby.

"And so?" we asked.

"Well, he was killed in battle."

"A lot of people killed in battle are buried there," I reminded Bobby.

"This one is different."

"How so?" Corky asked.

"He died from a hand grenade blast in his face."

"So?"

"People say they have seen him at night with his hands covering his face."

"And then?"

"When he comes closer, he puts his hands down."

"And?"

"He doesn't have a face."

"Ohhhhhhh," we moaned.

"Hey, what we going to do with all of the leftovers?" asked my brother, Jimmy.

"I don't want it," said Andy. "Any of you guys want it?"

"Heck, just throw it in the bushes. The cats and the dogs or mongoose will eat it eventually," said Lloyd.

"Did all of you guys bring your flashlights?" asked Tommy. "Shine the flashlights in the face of any stranger during the night. If it's not someone you recognize, attack with your swords, you hear?"

"Don't worry. We know what to do," we shouted. Earlier in the day we had shaped pieces of wood into swords as weapons to defend ourselves. Yes, we were certainly brave boys, full of bravado and courage, as long as there was daylight to protect us from the sinister monster called night.

There is no boy who has grown up in a small town who has not gone camping. We were no different from other boys growing up in small towns throughout America. Camping is the first break from parental control. It is a sign of independence. It is the beginning of the dash for freedom that all young men seek. It is a rite of passage. It is an educational process when you learn of things sitting around the campfire not taught in school books. It is a wonderful transitional activity for young boys.

The best part of camping like all other youthful, and even adult, activities is the planning, the discussions, looking forward to the good times we expected to have. Like many things in life, talking about doing something is just as enjoyable, if not more enjoyable, as actually doing that something. The journey is as much fun as reaching the destination.

One day in early July, while seated on the branches of the guava tree that stood in the far corner of my father's farm located in the back of our home, Corky came up with a brilliant idea. "You know what we should do one day?" he asked to no one in particular.

Nobody answered because we all knew that Corky would eventually answer his own question.

"You know what would be really fun to do?" he continued. "I mean really fun?"

Still no one responded, not that we were rude. Silence at a time like this was also a form of communication. With one person talking and the rest of us remaining silent was a dialogue between speaker and the silent majority, who did not wish to appear overly excited with whatever Corky's idea was. We appeared somewhat blasé to anyone's idea.

"We should go camping, that's what we should do."

Tommy asked the natural question, "And where do you think we should go camping?"

"How about the beach somewhere?" suggested Andrew.

"That's too much of a humbug. Someone has to take us there and then an adult would have to be with us. The police wouldn't allow kids to be at the park without any chaperon."

"We could go to the country," said Tommy. You could tell he was really into the idea of going camping. In fact, we all were, without admitting it.

"Nah, same thing. An adult would have to come along with us. We want this to be only us, no adults. It's our idea. It's no fun with adults around," said Corky.

"I know where we could go without any chaperon," said Lloyd.

"Where?" we all hollered.

"Right there," he said.

"Right there, where?" we all piped up. Sometimes, it's hard to figure out something that is so obvious. "Right there, underneath the old avocado tree." Lloyd pointed toward the direction of the tree.

"Shoot, that's no fun," said my brother, Jimmy. "We always play there. There's nothing different about camping underneath the old avocado tree. Another thing, it's too close to home."

"Think about it. We could sleep in the tents and cook our meals over a fire, just like the way we do it in the Cub Scouts," suggested Corky. "Our parents wouldn't object because we wouldn't be far from home."

"Hey, I think it's a great idea," I interjected.

We all scampered down the tree and ran home to get our equipment, our food, our flashlights and our parents' consent.

As the day began to fade and the long shadows of dusk slowly turned to night, we could see the faint outline of my father coming toward us with something in his hands.

"I wonder why my father is coming?" I asked.

"I wonder what he has in his hands?" Andy asked.

When my father reached the campsite, he asked, "How you boys doing? Is everything OK?"

"We're all fine. No problem, Dad," I answered. "What's that you have?"

"You boys might get hungry, and so, you can have some chocolate cake later," he said.

"That's really nice, Mr. Kodani," the boys yelled out.

"If you boys need anything during the night, you know where we live," he said with a smile. "Have fun."

"Don't worry, we will be fine," Jimmy replied.

As it grew darker, we threw more logs onto the campfire, and yet, now blanketed by a shroud of darkness, there seemed to be an arctic chill in the air. We huddled close together.

"Hey, what about the ghost stories?" asked Andrew.

"You guys tell yours first," replied Tommy.

"Mine can wait until later," said Corky.

"How about we all wait awhile," suggested Lloyd.

The enthusiasm for ghost stories had died out. We threw more logs onto the fire. It was a nice blazing fire, and yet, strangely, we shivered in the summer darkness. We all stared at the fire without saying a word. I didn't dare look toward the cemetery. I was afraid of what I might see. I know the others felt the same. The cemetery and everything connected with the cemetery were very much on our minds. When you really think about it, the dead in the cemetery can't do much to us, the living. They are safer than the living. They certainly can't cause us physical harm. They can't harass us. They can't annoy us. You would think they are perfectly harmless. They are, but not their presence. The fear of the dead disturbs our minds and emotions. The perception of ghosts like other perceptions is usually blown way out of proportion to its reality. The unknown is a terrible thing.

"Heeeeeeey. Is it my imagination, or is that something I see there in the cemetery?" asked Thomas.

We turned to look. I certainly couldn't see anything from my half-closed eyes like watching a scary movie at the theater. "It's just your imagination," I answered as bravely as I could.

"Are you sure?" he asked. "Don't you see something going back and forth in the cemetery?"

Good grief. I wasn't sure, but I wasn't going there to confirm his suspicions.

"How about some cake?" I asked.

The answers varied. "Not hungry right now." "Later." "I'll pass." Under ordinary circumstances, we would have devoured any dessert. Fear has a way of cutting down one's appetite.

Out in the open, even with a bright campfire and the soft moonlight, the night seemed darker than usual. On that particular night, the darkness was stifling. By now, we were hypersensitive of everything around us. We were so afraid we could hardly breathe. The blackness of night was claustrophobic. Electricity is such an integral part of modern life that we don't truly appreciate it until we are without it. Electricity not only gives us sufficient light at night, but it wards off all the fears caused by darkness. The brightness of the light keeps the monsters of the night at bay. I can't imagine how it must have been in the days of lamps and candles. The dim light must have made the nights darker, lonelier, scarier.

"I'm going into the tent," said Corky.

That was the best idea yet. No one objected.

Now, we were huddled in the tent. Each of us deep in our own private thoughts. At about this time, we preferred being in the safety and comfort of our homes. We had come this far. We had our pride to uphold. We couldn't back out now. Plus, we were going to have fun and an enjoyable time. This was to be the adventure of our lifetime. I thought there was nothing to worry about.

Suddenly, we heard sounds. Sounds close by.

"What's that?" someone whispered.

No one answered.

The sounds came closer and closer. It wasn't footsteps, for sure. Something was moving about, but what was it? There was some rustling in the bushes nearby. My mind raced with all kinds of thoughts. Could it be ghosts, I wondered. Was it the old lady with white hair wearing a white dress without any feet? Was this why we couldn't hear footsteps? I had giant goose bumps all over. And talk about cold sweat.

We didn't dare move. I was not too sure of that "something" in the cemetery, but I was definitely sure of the sounds approaching us. Something was headed our way. I was positive it was not our imagination.

About six to seven feet away from us, that something paused momentarily. My heart stopped beating. Then, that something sort of sniffed and yelped with a primitive growl.

We screamed our heads off. "Ahhhhhhhhhhhh!!!" We yelled out like we had never yelled out before. We were babbling like fools. "What should we do? What should we do?" We were no longer intelligible. We were going out of our wits. The ghosts were around us and upon us. "Help! Help!" We were going crazy with fear. We were hysterical. We didn't know whether to remain in the tents, or to run for our lives from the camp to our homes. We couldn't think straight. We couldn't even think, period. Cold chills ran up and down my spine, and back up and down several times. My legs were weak. I was drenched with cold sweat.

"I think I going to pee in my pants," someone said in the darkness of the tent. I knew exactly how he felt. I was shaking uncontrollably. All my vital organs were going berserk with fear and apprehension.

We were terrified. I was convinced of one thing. We were not quite ready for freedom and independence. We needed our parents, for sure.

I couldn't take it anymore. I said, "Let's get out of here! Let's go home!" No one objected. I bolted from the tent. The others followed, very close behind. We fled, each to the sanctuary our own homes.

We raced across the field in the darkness. We didn't need the flashlights. We had no use for our wooden swords. What use is a sword against a ghost? Like the ghost without feet, our feet moved so fast that they hardly touched the ground. We didn't dare to look back. We were chased away. Yes, we were chased by our own fears. Fears created by ourselves.

Mama! Daddy! Open that door! We're coming home.

As we dashed into the living room, my father asked, "Did you forget something, Roy?"

"Oh, we just decided to come home, Dad," I said as nonchalantly as I could under the circumstances.

"What's the matter? Did something happen? You're out of breath, both of you."

"Oh, nothing."

"Why did you come home?"

"The others decided to go home, and so, we thought we should come home too."

"You boys didn't stay out too long."

"What time is it, Dad?" I asked.

"Not quite eight o'clock."

Not quite eight o'clock? I couldn't believe it. It seemed like we had spent an eternity under the stars.

"Did you boys enjoy the cake?" my mother asked.

In all the excitement, I had forgotten about the cake. "Well, actually, we didn't even touch the cake," I said.

"Daddy, I think you'd better go and get it. It would be a waste to leave it there," she said.

My father was not gone for more than ten minutes. When he returned, he said, "You boys must have thrown food around the camp. There were dogs there, eating the food you had thrown in the bushes."

So that was it. There had been no ghosts. There was a logical explanation for the sounds we had heard. If only we had taken the time to investigate, we would have learned that the sounds were just the neighborhood dogs. They were eating the leftovers we had scattered in the bushes after dinner.

Whenever I think about that camping incident, I recall we were crazed by fear. A fear of the unknown. By nightfall, we had psyched ourselves into believing that something evil was bound to happen to us. There was no need to spook us with ghost stories. We had spooked ourselves. President Franklin D. Roosevelt was right when he wisely said, "There is no fear except fear itself." ◗

THE CRAZY OLD LADY

I f you should ever see a Japanese movie, often times you will hear the distinctive melancholy chords of the musical string instrument called *koto* as background music. It is like a long, narrow harp about six to eight feet long laid on the floor with the player sitting beside it, playing with both hands. One hand to pluck and the other to press the strings. The sound is uniquely Japanese just as the sound of the bagpipe is uniquely Scottish. Even today, when I hear the sounds of the koto I recall a particularly amazing woman whose personality changed dramatically before my eyes.

Among the *issei* (first-generation) Japanese-American women in Hawai'i, she was a most unusual woman. She was a highly cultured person. She was educated and, wonder of wonders, she spoke impeccable English at a time when even the second-and third-generation Asians in Hawai'i continued to speak pidgin English. In my elementary school days whenever she spoke to me, the regal way she carried herself, her elegant mannerisms and her soft, feminine voice intimidated me.

She was the grandmother of my friend, Stanley, and because of how this story will unfold, I must keep her identity confidential. I shall refer to her as Mrs. C.

Since she was not like the older women I knew at that time, I once asked my mother, "Ma, why is Mrs. C so different from the other women? I mean she is about the same age as Grandma but she is sure different from Grandma, or other women her age? How come, Ma?"

"Well, for one thing, she is a real lady."

"What do you mean a real lady? She's not a man, Ma."

I was very fortunate to have parents who were patient, who were willing to explain things to me. I should be as patient as they were.

"Mrs. C is not like other women who wear fancy clothes and expensive jewelry and think they are ladies. Mrs. C is the oldest daughter of the first son of an old family in Tokyo. Her father, as I understand, was a high-ranking politician. As the daughter of a prominent family, she learned all the things that the wife of a high-ranking person was supposed to know. Most of the women of Grandma's generation who came to Hawai'i were poor, and because they were poor, they had immigrated to Hawai'i to seek a better life. That was not true in Mrs. C's case."

"If she was such a big shot lady, holy maloney, why did she leave such a wonderful life and come to Hawai'i?"

"Because of Stanley's grandfather, who was also a very unusual man. He came to Hawai'i as a contract laborer to work in the sugarcane fields like most Asian men. But, he was different in a way. I understand that he was the son of a school teacher in Japan, and because of that he had more education than the poor people who came to Hawai'i. After working three years and finishing his contract, he became an independent sugar grower, which was highly unusual in those days. There weren't too many Oriental independent sugar growers. Yet, by hard work and a good business sense, he was able to save enough money to lease land, hire workers and plant sugarcane. In five to six years, he was a successful sugar planter."

"Where does Stanley's grandmother come in?" I asked.

"Stanley's grandfather eventually got married," my mother answered.

"That's where Mrs. C comes in?"

"No, Stanley's grandfather got married to another woman."

"You mean he was married to two women?"

"No. Of course not, Roy. He first married the daughter of a sugar plantation *luna* (foreman), and their marriage was a very happy one. They had four children, and while giving birth to the fifth child, Stanley's first grandmother died. In those days, sad to say, quite a number of women died in childbirth."

"It must have been rough for Stanley's grandfather."

"Oh, yes, it certainly was. He tried to manage by hiring a housekeeper, but it was too much for him. He had to take care of a family of four young children and a baby. At the same time, he had to handle all of his business as a sugar planter."

"Is this where Mrs. C comes in?"

"Not right away. Stanley's grandfather wrote to his parents in Japan asking that they find a suitable wife for him, someone who would be a good mother to his five children. You couldn't expect a young woman to leave the comforts of her home and travel thousands of miles to Hawai'i to raise five children. I don't think there are too many young women today who would be willing to take care and raise five young children, especially if the children are not her own. His parents politely asked and finally, they pleaded, and still no one showed any interest in coming to Hawai'i and marrying Stanley's grandfather."

"So, how does Mrs. C come into the picture?"

"Five or six months later, a young woman was visiting her aunty in the village where Stanley's grandfather was living, and she heard that a young man with five children was looking for a wife in faraway Hawai'i. She didn't even know where Hawai'i was then. Maybe she felt sorry for the children, maybe she was seeking an adventure, maybe she wanted to do good in a far off land, maybe a lot of others things. Whatever may have been the reason, she returned to the city and asked her parents if she could marry Stanley's grandfather. They said that she was young and foolish to even consider the idea. She didn't give up. She persisted, and her parents finally gave in. Stanley's grandfather arranged for her to travel by ship over to Hawai'i, and on her arrival in Honolulu, she married Stanley's grandfather in a quiet Shinto shrine ceremony."

"I'm glad to hear that, but why do you take so long to get to the point, Ma?"

"Well, the story doesn't end there."

"How come? Stanley's grandfather married Mrs. C, didn't he? What else did he have to do?"

"Just be a little patient and I'll be able to finish the whole story."

"I can't imagine what else is involved."

"If you'll just let me finish, I can get on with the story, Roy. As it happened, Stanley's grandfather and grandmother weren't married for even half a year when a great tragedy struck."

"What happened?"

"In those days, the sugar planters supervised their workmen and checked the sugar fields by riding around on a large work horse, not the smaller quarter horses. Stanley's grandfather did the same. On this particular day, as Stanley's grandfather was getting off his horse, something suddenly spooked the horse, and before he could get off the horse, it bucked and started to gallop at full speed. It would have been better if Stanley's grandfather had been thrown off his horse, but he wasn't. His foot got caught on the stirrups, and he couldn't get back on the horse. He was hanging upside down. He tried his best to get back on, but the more he struggled, the more the horse panicked. The horse dragged Stanley's grandfather along the road, filled with rocks and stones and cinders. The workmen saw what was happening and they all tried to stop the horse, but the horse raced on like a mad demon. The horse was crazed with fear. People have told me that the horse galloped at full speed for about a mile or two before the workmen chased it into the thick bushes. By then, Stanley's grandfather was battered beyond recognition. His head was like a pulp. Just terrible. I understand that he didn't die immediately. He suffered in great agony for about a day or two and finally died."

"What did Mrs. C do?"

"Well, it was almost too much for her to handle. Just imagine, a young woman in her early twenties, in a foreign land, a widow with five young children who were not her own. I once told her that I had nothing but admiration for her. I told her I would have gone crazy. Mrs. C said at first she was in a state of shock, feeling helpless, frustrated, angry. The priest who conducted her husband's funeral told her that no one would think bad of her if she were to take the children back to Japan to her husband's family. After all, they were all her husband's children, not her own. She was tempted to do that. That would have been the easiest thing for her to do, but she realized that her husband would not have wanted her to do that. She felt that it was her duty and responsibility to raise the children."

"Would you have done that, Ma?"

"It would have been very, very hard, Roy. I really don't know what I would have done in such a case. She also realized that she could not handle the work of a sugar planter, after all, she was a woman, and no man would have worked for a woman in those days, especially, a young, inexperienced woman. So, she sold the sugarcane fields."

"I bet she made lots of money, huh, Ma. Didn't she?"

"Unfortunately, no. The other sugar planters were able to buy the sugarcane land very cheaply because she had no other choice but to sell the land. You make a profit when others want to buy your property, not when you are forced to sell anything. After she paid off the debts and expenses, there wasn't much left for her and the children. She felt she was in a hopeless situation. She said she was raised to be strong and to adapt to the worse of situations."

"So, what did she do? Did she go on welfare or something?"

"No, she did not. In fact, there was no welfare assistance in those days. And knowing Mrs. C, even if there were welfare, I don't think she would have gone on welfare. She is a proud woman. No, she decided to become a Japanese language school teacher, and that's what she became. With her meager salary, she educated all of the children, each and every one of them. They all received a college education when a college education was difficult for even a man to provide his children."

By the late 1940s, when Stanley and I were friends, Mrs. C was retired and was living with Stanley and his parents. I would go to Stanley's home and play with him, and Stanley in turn would come to my home and would stay all day. Stanley's home was different from the rest of the other homes I visited. I guess it was because of his grandmother, Mrs. C, that they had very nice things in their home. They had Japanese scrolls hanging on the wall, antique vases, Japanese dolls, ceramic pieces. As you entered the front door, the first thing you saw was the photograph of a very stern-looking Asian man with a huge, thick mustache. This was Mr. C. In that photograph, Mr. C looked more Caucasian than Japanese. The handlebar mustache may have made the difference.

After an hour or two of playing outside, Mrs. C would call us in and, as refined a lady as she was, would serve Stanley and me sugar cookies and milk.

"How are you today, Roy?" she would always ask me.

"Very well, thank you, Mrs. C," I would murmur.

"How is your mother and father?" she would then ask.

"Fine," I would respond.

"Will you please give your parents my regards," she would next say.

"Yes," I would say. Coming from Mrs. C, I felt it as a command, and so, duty bound, I would always tell my parents, "Hey, Ma, Daddy, Stanley's grandmother said to give you her regards. OK?"

My mother would say, "Please be sure to tell Mrs. C that I should visit her, but I have been busy helping Daddy at the store, but that one of these days, I will be sure to visit her."

"Gee, do I have to? I really feel uncomfortable talking to her. It's like talking to a school teacher."

"She was a school teacher. It's good for you, Roy. You should talk to people who speak well. It's good experience for you."

However, whenever I went to Stanley's home, I just couldn't repeat to her what my mother had instructed me to say. It seemed too much for me to say. I just answered what she asked. I was fidgety in her presence.

I once asked Stanley, "Stan, how come your grandmother speaks English so well?"

"It's because as a young girl in Japan she was a student in a girl's Catholic school, taught by English nuns or something like that."

It was during those days when I would visit Stanley that I would hear Mrs. C playing the koto. Whenever she did, I could not help but to stop whatever I was doing and listen for a while as she played. Though I may have been young, I could sense her feelings as she played. Slow and mournful when she was sad, light and playful when she was happy. The music reflected her moods. Even today, when I hear the sounds of the koto I recall Mrs. C sitting in the living room totally concentrating on the koto.

As the years went on, inevitably things changed and one change that came about was Mrs. C. One Saturday, late in the afternoon, Stanley's mother invited me to dinner, "Roy, why don't you stay for dinner? Maybe you should telephone your mother and say that you will be staying for dinner. We will take you home after dinner."

When I telephoned my mother, she said, "You may stay for dinner, but behave yourself. Don't talk nonsense. And remember our family matters are private matters. You don't have to tell everybody what our family does and says. Do you understand? Be sure to say thank you. Don't talk at the table unless the adults talk to you. After dinner, be sure to take your plate to the sink, and offer to wash the dishes. I don't want Stanley's mother and grandmother to think that we didn't raise you properly. Always have good manners."

"OK, Ma, OK. Hurry up, I gotta go."

"Be sure to thank Stanley's mother for inviting you to dinner. Don't forget, Roy."

During dinner, a strange thing happened. At first, I couldn't quite understand what was happening. This was the first of a series of bizarre things involving Mrs. C that I experienced.

As we were eating, Mrs. C pointed to the salt, "Please pass me the—the—the—"

I looked at the salt and then looked at Mrs. C. At first, I thought she was joking, but she was not the type of person to joke.

She stabbed the air with her forefinger. "You know what I mean. That white thing, that white thing."

I knew she was talking about the salt, but I wondered why she just couldn't come out and say "salt."

Stanley's father quietly said, "*Okasan* (mother), you mean the salt, don't you?"

"Yes, yes, the salt." She was frustrated because she couldn't remember the word "salt."

I thought, *Oh, well, she must be getting old and forgetful.*

At that time, it was not a big thing and I let it pass.

A month or two later, as Stanley and I were tossing the baseball, Mrs. C stepped out on the porch and called out to Stanley, "Ichiro! Ichiro!"

Stanley looked at Mrs. C and stood there with the ball in his hand.

"Who is she calling?" I asked.

"She's calling my dad. She thinks I'm my dad," he answered. How could that be, I wondered.

In late spring, I went to Stanley's home because we were going to pick mountain apples near his home. When I arrived, the police were there. I thought, *Wow! What is happening?*

I walked up the stairs and peeked in. Stanley saw me. He pulled me out. "You know what happened?"

"No, what happened?" I responded.

"My grandmother..." he started to say.

I thought the worst. "Someone killed her."

"No. No one killed her. She's missing."

"What do you mean missing?"

"She's missing."

"Did someone kidnap her?"

"No, you fool. Why should anyone kidnap my grandmother? She is not rich or anything."

"Then, how did it happen? You don't get up one morning and find your grandmother missing."

"Roy, honest to god, when we got up in the morning, she didn't come to the kitchen. Usually, she is the first one down to breakfast, but this morning she wasn't in the kitchen when my mother got up, and so, she went to look for Grandma and she was not in her room. She was nowhere in the house. We looked for her everywhere outside, and still we couldn't find her. She just disappeared."

"That's weird, Stan. I mean someone just doesn't disappear. She must be somewhere."

"That's what my father said too. It's kinda embarrassing, but we had to call the police to help us find her."

Inside, the police officers were asking Stanley's mother and father all kinds of questions about Mrs. C. Had she been depressed recently? No. Did she have any health problems? No. Did she have any money problems? No. Had they offended her in any way? Not that they could remember. Had she disappeared before? No. Maybe she got up early and went to see someone? If she did, she would certainly have told them about it the night before.

The phone suddenly rang. It was another police officer. They had found Mrs. C wandering around about a mile away. They would bring her home. Everyone was relieved. Except that when the police car arrived and the officer escorted her into the house, everyone gasped. Mrs. C, who was always properly dressed, was only wearing a slip. I just couldn't look at her. I mumbled something to Stanley and I quietly left.

That was the beginning of many other times when Mrs. C would leave the house and would be found half-dressed wandering around the neighborhood. The other kids would taunt her and call her "Crazy Old Lady." To me, it was very sad. Finally, Stanley's parents had to lock her up in her room. She became very forgetful. There were times when she would remember me, but most times, she thought I was someone else. As time went on, she would become hysterical and rant and rave. She was now an entirely different woman.

When Stanley turned ten years old, he had a birthday party, and he invited me to spend the night with him. I wasn't too keen about it, but after all, Stanley and I were good friends, and so, I accepted. Stanley's parents were very gracious. They made me feel at home. All through the party and throughout the evening, I didn't see nor hear Mrs. C. With all the excitement of the party, Stanley and I were tired and we feel asleep about ten o'clock.

I must have been sleeping very deeply because at first I thought I was dreaming. I heard someone playing the koto, like a professional koto musician, like a virtuoso, like I had heard Mrs. C play the koto many years ago before she lost her memory. It was totally unreal. At first, I listened without opening my eyes. I wondered whether it was a dream or was this for real?

Stanley stirred and said, "That's my grandmother playing again."

"Your grandmother? But, I thought she can't remember anything? How can she remember the music?"

"I don't know how she does it, but she can remember how to play the koto."

I couldn't understand how she could be so forgetful and yet, remember how to play the koto. Stanley had told me that his parents were having a difficult time with his grandmother because she was like a child, and yet, in the middle of the night, she was playing a beautiful, lamenting piece on her koto.

As the years went on, Stanley and I made new friends and we went our separate ways in junior high school. It took a terrible toll on Stanley's mother caring for Mrs. C, who was difficult to handle and behaved like a child. The amazing thing about Mrs. C was that she remained physically fit for many years. Only her mind had degenerated.

During those years, when I was young, the fragility of the human body and the human mind was not obvious to me. I expected life to go on as it always did. It is only after you have experienced and seen how fragile we all are that you are deeply thankful for all the little blessings which we receive each day.

When I think about it now, almost forty years since the night she had played the koto, I am convinced she was not a crazy old lady. Mrs. C simply suffered from an illness. Mrs. C was the victim of Alzheimer's disease. At that time, we didn't know much about it. I have learned since then that a person afflicted with Alzheimer's disease cannot remember current matters (short-term memory) but, somehow, remembers things long past, years ago. And this is why Mrs. C could play the koto without any difficulty when her memory for all intents and purposes was gone. ◆

GONE FOREVER

"Daddy, Peter and Margaret have invited us to their baby daughter's birthday party Sunday. Why don't we go?" suggested my mother. "The children have never ridden on a train. I'm sure the children would enjoy the train ride. We could take the train to Laupāhoehoe, and Peter could pick us up at the train station there. More people are owning cars, and the railroad company is not doing too well financially. You never know, someday, the trains may not run on this island, Daddy."

"Hmmmm. Let me think about it. I'm busy at the store, and I'm busy on the farm. The tomatoes are ready to be harvested. Your brothers are coming to help me harvest on the weekends. I just can't go off to a party while they are working."

For almost ten years during the 1940s and early 1950s, my father had leased three acres of land in the back of our home on Kapiolani Street to do some farming on a part-time basis. He would work on the farm after working at the store and on weekends. Besides tomatoes, he also grew taro, green onions, peanuts, Chinese potato and carrots. One year he raised carnations. That year, my brother and I had the fanciest leis on May Day at school, because my father, being very imaginative, had combined all the different colored carnations into a strand of lei. At the May Day event at Hilo Union School, all the teachers ooohed and ahhhed because our leis were so colorful. They had never seen such multicolored leis at that time. My parents also raised chickens, ducks and turkeys. Under the present zoning laws regulating the use of land, they certainly couldn't have had a mini-farm in a residential neighborhood as they did in those days.

"I can talk to my brothers and explain to them. You have never taken a day off from work, Daddy. I know they will understand if you took one day off. This is something special too. I know Peter and Margaret would appreciate if we joined them. We have been their friends for so long, way before even Roy was born. Let me talk to my brothers, Daddy?"

"No. I don't believe in going off for pleasure while others are working. I don't like to do things like that. Call Margaret and tell her we're sorry we can't make it, but after the tomato harvest season we'll go and visit them. It may be later, but you know what they say, 'Better late, than never.' I'm sure Peter will understand. After all, he's an agriculture teacher at Laupāhoehoe School."

"Daddy, let's go for the children's sake. You have to relax sometimes."

"As I said, Mama, we will go, but not this time, later."

A few weeks later, as the sun set on March 31, 1946, I can still recall hearing a sound I had never before heard. In the darkening sky, I heard the low, mournful cawing and screeching of seagulls and albatrosses. It sounded like thousands of restless seabirds swirling in the sky. I peered in the darkness hoping to get a glimpse of the birds, but they were so high in the sky, I could not see them.

My mother after doing the dinner dishes, wiping her wet hands on her apron, came out and listened to the cry of the birds and said, "A bad storm must be coming. Seabirds come inland when they know the sea will be rough."

"How do the birds know," I asked.

"Somehow, the birds know," my mother answered.

The next morning, Monday, April 1, 1946, April Fools' Day, began like any other normal day. I got up, had breakfast around seven o'clock and then went out to the chicken coop to help my mother feed the chickens.

The quiet of the early morning was shattered by my father running up to us shouting, "Mama, Mama, we've been hit by a *tsunami* (tidal wave)! We have already been hit one or two times."

"What happened, Daddy?" my mother asked.

"I was at the store getting ready to open for business, when I heard people shouting. I couldn't quite understand what they were saying at first. Loud voices. Screaming and yelling. Something really bad was happening, especially by the ocean. People were running all round town. There was a lot of commotion. Then I heard, 'Tsunami! Run away! Run away! Tsunami! Tsunami!' I ran to the corner of Keawe and Mamo Streets. I looked toward the ocean. Oh my god! You should see it. The high waves had destroyed several buildings. I couldn't believe it. There were huge boulders scattered all over Kamehameha Avenue (the front street parallel to the ocean). Can you believe that? Huge, huge boulders. They must have rolled in with the waves. Maybe from the breakwater."

"What are we going to do?" asked my mother.

I was worried the tidal waves would destroy our home located about a mile from the bay front on a higher elevation.

"Daddy, did you think it'll come here?" I asked.

"I don't think so, Roy, I don't think so, at least, I hope not." That wasn't too assuring.

My father was also worried about his brother, Stanley, who had his tailor shop on Kamehameha Avenue. "I'd better hurry," he said. "I'll take my truck and help him. If this keeps up, he'll have nothing left."

"Be careful, whatever you do, Daddy. I know you must help your brother, but don't take any chances. If you must run away to save your life, please run."

Meanwhile, about thirty miles north of Hilo in Laupāhoehoe, jutting out to sea is a low, level peninsula, the remnant of an ancient lava flow. On that disastrous day, the Laupāhoehoe Elementary School stood there. Before the first wave struck at about seven o'clock, the waters receded far out to sea, sucked by a tremendous force caused by a major earthquake about four hours earlier off the coast of Alaska. It was as though someone had pulled the ocean plug and all the water had flowed down the ocean drain. The school children, who had arrived early, had never in their lives seen anything like this. The ocean floor lay bare before them. There were fishes floundering helplessly everywhere along the now barren coast. For many of the children, feeling simultaneously a sense of curiosity and a sense of foreboding evil, curiosity prevailed. They dashed headlong toward the sea hoping to catch the fishes flopping everywhere as far as the eye could see. As they were laughing and squealing with delight at what they thought was their good fortune for having arrived so early to school, monster waves measuring twenty to thirty feet, maybe higher, barreled into shore, sounding much like a thousand runaway freight trains weighted down by a load of hell-bent, violent energy. As the waves crashed onto land with a thunderous boom, the children looked up with horror. This was totally incomprehensible. The normally placid coastal waters were now a diabolic sea of destruction. They fled as fast as they could, hoping to escape the clutch of the on-rushing monster waves. With the waves travelling at a speed of approximately 500 miles per hour across the Pacific Ocean, what chance did those children have?

About a hundred yards from the school were the teachers' cottages where most of the teachers lived with their families. Many of the teachers would spend their summers away from Laupāhoehoe, and some were already making plans for their summer vacation although it was still about two and a half months away. Teaching at a school like Laupāhoehoe was an idyllic experience for many. It was a close-knit sugar plantation community, with supportive and appreciative parents and well-behaved children.

Peter and Margaret had been school teachers here for about four years raising three young daughters; one, four, and seven years old. A young, bachelor school teacher, Frank, usually had breakfast with the family. As they were at the kitchen table, they heard the screaming and the yelling of the children.

"Why are the kids making all that noise?" asked Peter looking up from the table.

Margaret was feeding the baby. "Something's happening out by the water, Peter. Maybe you should go and check, don't you think?"

"Well, I can't imagine what it can be, so early in the morning."

"I'm almost finished, Peter. I'll go," said Frank.

"That reminds me. Today's April Fools' Day. Watch those kids. Maybe they're up to something. You know how these kids are, Frank."

"Oh my god!" cried Frank.

"What is it?" asked Peter.

"Peter, the ocean! The whole ocean! The whole ocean is coming in!"

Peter and Margaret stood instantly. They were mesmerized at what they saw. Already a huge wall of brown-blackish sea raced across the peninsula.

Frank yelled, "Run! Run! Just run for it!"

Margaret cried out, "Peter, the children. Grab the children!" As Peter attempted to scoop up the two older girls, the waves pounded the house and lifted it up from its foundation.

"Peter, where are you?" screamed Margaret in the wild, maelstrom of the angry sea. Peter reached out for Margaret. His fingers touched Margaret for a second. The rushing waters knocked him to the side.

"Margaret! Margaret!" he screamed.

Frank turned and grabbed the oldest daughter, Sarah, and the second oldest daughter, Stella, and held tightly onto both girls. The waters battered and dragged him down. He couldn't breathe. He gasped for air. At this rate, all three of them would drown and none of them would make it. Reluctantly, ever so reluctantly, without making a conscious choice or a decision as to why, he let go of Stella. The waves rolled him and Sarah like children's dolls across the stretch of land, now filled with sand, broken, lumber and debris. At his first chance, taking a deep breath, he touched his feet to the ground. As the waters receded again with a deep swoosh, he scampered toward the higher elevation with Sarah still in his grasp.

"Mommy, Mommy, I want Mommy," she whimpered.

Frank looked toward the sea. He could see heads bobbing in the tumultuous sea. Some were crying out, "Help! Help! Save me!" The lucky ones were rescued in time. Stories were later told of others who drowned. More terrifying, were stories of sharks being sighted in the angry waters.

Meanwhile, Peter was tossed by the wave and caught between a tree and a boulder. He, too, survived, but Margaret and the other two daughters were never found.

Back in town, my father and Uncle Stanley were loading up the truck with as many sewing machines as they possibly could. On that day a series of tidal waves came crashing in, some more terrible and destructive than others. Years later, those who were caught in it and survived to tell about it, would talk about the third wave, or the fourth wave, or the eighth wave, as if each wave had a destructive personality of its own. The town of Hilo is situated on a crescent-shaped bay, and consequently, the bay acts like a funnel with the tidal waves rushing in with tremendous force into a narrow area.

"Watch out! Wave coming!" someone yelled.

"Let's go," cried out my father.

"I'm going to get one more thing from the back," said Uncle Stanley.

"No time, Stanley. Let's go," yelled my father.

"Won't take long."

"Come on, Stanley. You'll lose everything."

"I gotta get it."

"You wanna die?"

They dashed to the truck and gunned the truck up the street with only seconds to spare as a giant wave surged in. Huge boulders weighing eight tons or more rolled in, sounding like monster bowling balls gone astray in the gutter, flying into the air like pebbles on the beach.

"My god, look, *Anisan* (older brother)," said Uncle Stanley. My father looked toward the sea. In the blink of an eye, most of the buildings along Front Street were destroyed. Only the foundations could be seen.

After my father had left, I asked my mother, "Ma, can I go and see the waves, huh, Ma?"

"Go to the corner. Don't roam around now. Do you understand?"

By the time I ran to the corner, I could hear people saying, "OOOOOO!" There was a large crowd gathered looking toward the sea. In Hilo Bay, there is a little island the size of a football stadium called Coconut Island located not far from the mouth of Wailoa River. As I stood and watched, a massive wave rolled from the north and washed over Coconut Island and smashed into Shinmachi, a community of closely packed homes near the mouth of Wailoa River. Then, a minute or two later, I saw houses and boats floating in the bay. The devastation of the tsunami was awesome. Shinmachi was completely destroyed, and to this day, no home has ever been rebuilt in that district.

In some places on the island, the waves came in as far as one half-mile inland. Two hours later, at about nine o'clock in the morning, when the last wave washed in, 500 homes or businesses had been totally destroyed and 1000 others were damaged. The total amount of destruction was $26,000,000, which in today's dollar value would be almost ten times that amount.

By the end of that April Fools' Day, a cruel joke on Hawai'i, ninety-six people had died including sixteen children and five teachers at Laupāhoehoe, hundreds more hurt, thousands emotionally and psychologically scared forever. The tidal waves of 1946 caused the slow death of the sugar industry on the island of Hawai'i. The day before the tidal waves was the high-water mark of the sugar industry on the island. From that day on, the once mighty sugar industry was never to recover fully. The tsunami destroyed an orderly and predictable social order. An entire civilization, to exaggerate a bit, which had taken several generations of hard labor to build was wiped out and gone forever in a matter of two hours.

Rails were torn off the railroad beds. Bridges were washed away by the tidal waves. An entire leg of a high steel railroad trestle was twisted off its base and carried far upstream. In Hilo, at the mouth of Wailuku River, a span of the railroad bridge was torn off by the power of the massive waves and deposited on a lava outcropping called Maui's Canoe and was to remain there for two decades as a reminder of that fateful day. It was estimated that the force of the water in some places attained the pressure of 2,000 pounds per square foot. The cost of rebuilding the railroad system was too high, bringing to an end in one day a railroad industry, which had been responsible to a large degree for the success and prosperity of sugar in Hawai'i. In short, my brother, sister and I never had the chance of riding the railroad train on our island.

To prevent another similar tragedy, which had struck with absolutely no warning, the Pacific Tsunami Warning System was established in the late 1940s.

A year after the tsunami destruction, we all attended a memorial service conducted by the community association of Laupāhoehoe. As we approached the clearing where the school once stood, my father said, "I guess sometimes we shouldn't wait for a better time to do something we always intend to do. If we wait, we may never have the chance of getting around to do what we always plan to do later."

It was a picture-perfect kind of day—warm sun, blue sky, fleecy white clouds on the horizon, the gentle waves lapping the shore lazily, children running around after the service. It was hard to believe that a year earlier, a tragedy of unimaginable terror had occurred on this same plot of land. By then, the elementary school had been moved up to higher grounds. A stone memorial with the names of all those who died are inscribed on the plaque, located near where the school once stood. For years my parents would go to the Laupāhoehoe tidal wave memorial and place lit *senko* (joss sticks) at the memorial. As the white smoke curled heavenward, I used to wonder if the souls of the people who died were now at peace, after such a terrifying experience. ◖

OYAKOKO

We all called him Taisho (General), which was not his real name; I didn't know his real name until later. He was four years older than I, and in those days four years was a vast difference.

I got to know Taisho, because we all used to play pick-up basketball at the Hilo Boarding School gym. If I recall correctly, the color of the exterior walls was red, and it was next to the home of the Shintaku family, located between the large, white Hilo Boarding School building and the gym.

Because it used to rain a lot in Hilo when I was growing up, there were gyms all over Hilo and in each plantation camp. Within walking distance from my home on Kapiolani Street, there was a gym at Hilo High School, Hilo Intermediate School, Hilo Boarding School, Hilo Armory and at Haili Church. There was an outside basketball court at Lincoln Park. When I was a Cub Scout, I used to play at Hilo Center, which was across from Hilo Theater. Boys who grew up in Hilo may not all have played for the Hilo High School Vikings basketball team, but most of us played basketball for recreation without adult supervision.

When I think about it now, we would all walk home after playing basketball drenched with sweat. No one showered after the games, and no one carried a towel to wipe off the sweat. And until we were in high school, all of us walked everywhere barefoot. I don't believe any of us had shoes to play basketball. I have tried to recall who owned a basketball, but I don't remember any of us ever carrying a basketball before or after the game. Maybe the ball was at the gyms where we played.

Among boys and men, some are natural born leaders. Even when we are young, boys tend to listen and follow the natural born leader. Usually, a natural born leader is superior in what he does, such as outstanding athleticism, have sound moral values...he does not cheat, lie nor take advantage of other boys, they do not brag nor show off. He leads by example. Taisho was a natural born leader, and all the boys liked to play pick-up basketball with him. Basketball is a rough sport, and often times, there is shoving, pushing and bumping, which are penalties, but it is still done. Taisho never engaged in such behavior.

Taisho lived about three or four miles from downtown Hilo and must have come to school and gone home either on the Hilo sampan bus or with his friends.

Usually Taisho was quiet and played smoothly and effortlessly, but there were times when I noticed that he played like a wild monster, as though enraged by some unknown, dark demon. His behavior became worse as he grew older. His rage must have affected his behavior in class, because one day after a game as I was heading home alone walking through the Hilo Boarding School campus, he came up to me and asked, "Kodani, where you going?"

I thought his question was odd, because he knew I always walked home after the games. "I'm going home. Why?"

"I go walk with you," he said. It seemed to me then that he was troubled by something. After walking in silence, he blurted out, "The principal wanna have my parents come to school tomorrow."

"What for?" I asked. In those days parents rarely, if ever, were asked to come to school. And if they did, it was usually a disciplinary problem. He didn't say anything, and I didn't pry or be *niele* (nosy).

We walked in silence until we reached the corner of Haili Street and Kapiolani Street, where the Haili Store used to be, and he asked, "Kodani, you wanna eat candy?"

Although a candy bar was about a nickel, most of us didn't have extra money to buy candy, and so, his offer sort of threw me off. "You sure you have enough money to buy me candy?" I asked.

"Yeah, no worry. I got money." We leaned against the wall of the store and ate our candy, maybe Baby Ruth.

"You think I should tell my mother and father?"

"You mean about tomorrow?"

"Yeah, my mother might come, but my old man nevah going come."

We finished our candy in silence and then Taisho just walked down the hill without saying a word. Asking his parents must have really weighed heavily on his mind.

My father usually closed his hardware store about 5 p.m. and we would all have dinner about 5:30. At the dinner table my father would talk about things that happened at the store during the day, and my brother, sisters and I would talk about things that happened in school. After dinner my father would go out into the yard and putter with his plants and *bonsai.* There was no television in Hilo yet, and if there was still daylight we would go out and play in the yard. As long as I can remember, my father did not scream, holler or yell at anyone. He had a good sense of humor, and my parents got along well. Life was good and peaceful in our family.

When I was a teenager, a popular hangout was the Dairy Queen at the crossroads of Kamehameha Avenue and Kanoelehua Avenue. I don't think McDonald's had yet come to Hawai'i. There would be a lot of teenagers there on the weekend. Only a few of us had our own cars, and so I would go with another classmate who would pick me up in his father's Jeep. One particular weekend while I was there, Taisho came with his friends, and after awhile he asked us, "Hey, you guys, you wanna play 21?" It wasn't blackjack...it was a game played with a basketball. Each player had two chances to shoot the ball into the hoops. If you scored on the first shot, it was two points, and the second shot was one point. Whoever made twenty-one points won.

Everyone asked, "Where we gonna play?"

"My house," was Taisho's answer.

And so we went to his house (the location I need to keep confidential for obvious reasons). Like many Hilo homes, there was a basket hammered to the garage, and we must have played about an hour, when his mother came out with a pitcher of orange and lime juice, both picked from their yard.

"Boy-san, go drink juice," she said to us. She was rather tall for a Japanese woman, about five feet, eight inches, slim and very fair. She was a pretty woman. I didn't know much about her then, and even today I don't know much about her.

As we were drinking juice and talking story, Hilo style in the garage, a man drove up in old truck and we moved aside to let him drive in. "That's my old man," Taisho spoke. He was thin and short. He had a stub of whiskers and his hair was unkempt. Everything about him was the opposite of Taisho's mother. Young as I was then, my immediate thought was, *Why did Taisho's mother marry this man?*

About no more than five minutes after he straggled into the house, I heard Taisho's father yell out, "Go get some beer!"

We could all hear his mother say, "*Otosan* (father), no more money for beer. No more money. You gotta understand."

"Shit! What you wen do wit' your pay?"

"I tell you every time. I have to buy food, pay for electricity, rent. Elroy needs school money." It was then that I learned that Taisho's real name was Elroy.

"Shaddup! Shaddup!" Then, to my horror, even though we were outside, I heard a loud slap and something being thrown.

"Otosan, Elroy's friends outside. No hit me today." *What! I* thought, *today? You mean, it wasn't only today?*

"Otosan, go stop. No hit me. Stop already," Taisho's mother was whimpering.

"Goddamn! My old man busting up my mother again," Taisho said in anger. "He goes crazy when he drinks. My mother takes a lot of abuse. Sometimes, he hits her so much she is black and blue all over. Frigging old man."

The other boys and I just froze. I don't know about the other boys, but this was the first time I had experienced a husband, or any other man, physically abusing a woman. Even now, I can recall how shocked I was. I was emotionally drained. It was then I realized how much all this trauma was affecting Taisho.

The irony of this situation was that a police officer lived next door to Taisho's home. Many years later, I told my father and mother about it, and my father said, "No matter how bad the husband is to the wife, the police never interfered in a family's affair in those days. The family things were always private. It was up to the family to handle their own problems, as best as they can. In those days, other husbands used to beat up their wives. We knew about them, but no one said anything. Some men were just drunks...others, I think, were frustrated and took it out on the poor wives. Terrible, but what could we do?"

Many years later, when I was a young attorney, I was at Trader Vic's, which used to be at the corner of King Street and Ward Avenue. It was a shack where the Honolulu Club now stands. It was a popular place where a lot of people gathered after work. As I recall, I was standing with a group of other young men waiting for a table, when I heard someone call out to me, "Hey, Kodani, howzit?"

I stared. He looked familiar. "You no remember me? Taisho."

He was taller and heavier now. In our brief moment, I learned he had gone into the Army after graduation, then went to a Mainland college and became an engineer. He was now one of the principals in a civil engineering firm in Honolulu.

I could not resist asking him, "Taisho, how's your mother?"

"A few years ago, she got a stroke. I think all the stress and strain and the abuse got to her. She is now half-paralyzed, the right side. She cannot do too much. She didn't want to, but I brought her to live with me here. That went put a strain on my marriage, and after a while, my wife divorced me. I had to choose between my mother and my wife. My wife no can understand all my mother's suffering. I had to take care of my mother."

After that, Taisho and I would get together to talk about the Hilo days. I learned that every day, he would go to his home and feed his mother at lunch. This went on for about ten or fifteen years. I once asked him, "Taisho, why don't you put your mother into a care home?"

"Kodani, you cannot be serious, huh, after all my mother went through? Would you put your mother in a care home, especially if she doesn't want to go?"

Till the very end, Taisho took care of his mother at his home. His conduct reflects the essence of *oyakoko* (filial piety) to care for your parents without complaint. ♦

DOUBLE WHAMMY

As far back as I could remember, every year a few days before New Year's Day, Lefty would visit us, bringing as a gift a chicken, dressed and ready to be cooked. Nowadays, chicken is no big deal. It can be bought every day of the year at the supermarket. In the 1940s, chicken was not as readily available as meat or fish, therefore, receiving a chicken was much appreciated.

Lefty was one of the friendliest men I had ever met. He was always smiling, pleasant to everyone. There never seemed to be a cloud over him. You would have thought his life had always been happy and free of any bad experience.

I learned as children do from overhearing bits and pieces of adult conversations that my paternal grandmother had raised Lefty for a while after his mother had died when he was very young. My father was like an older brother to him. By the time I was eight or nine years old, he had been married and had two children; a daughter, who was few years younger than I, and a son about three years old. They would tag along with Lefty on his annual visit to our home. As my father and Lefty would sit on the long, wide porch of our home and chat, Lefty's children would play with my brother, sister and me.

When it rained, and it would pour relentlessly in Hilo during the month of December, Lefty would stay the entire afternoon and pass the time with my father because he knew that my father could not work outdoors. My mother would serve beer and snacks to the men, and buttered Saloon Pilot crackers sprinkled with sugar and milk to us kids.

My father and Lefty would talk about everything under the sun, but they liked to reminisce the best. I would hear my father say to Lefty, "I'm glad to see that you have a better and happier life now. You had a very hard life when you were a young, eh, Lefty? How old were you when your mother died?"

Lefty would answer, "Gee, Anisan, I was very young. I must have been about three years old. About the same age as my son. I will always be grateful to you and your mother. She took care of me while my father worked. Your family was poor too, but your mother fed me and treated me like one of her own children. She used to say to my father, 'We must all help each other when someone needs help.'"

My father would continue, "I can still remember your mother. She was a pretty lady. If I remember, she had a dimple. She was nice to everyone. She was like the sunshine. She made you feel warm inside when she smiled at you. You remind me of your mother. She caught pneumonia, didn't she? That was so unfortunate. In those days, people died from pneumonia. I give your father credit. After your mother died, he went to work every day, no matter how hard it was."

"You don't have to tell me. My father was never the same after my mother died. I know he missed my mother, because late at night I could hear him sobbing quietly in the other room. When I would hear him cry, I would cover the blanket over my head and I would cry too, as softly as I could so that he would not hear me."

"I know your father remarried after a year or two, didn't he?"

"In a way, I guess he had to. It was tough for a man to raise a young boy while he had to work from early morning to late in the evening. He also needed someone to help him at home. It was too much for him to work as a plantation laborer in the cane fields and to come home and do the house chores. I know your mother would have gladly continued to raise me, but my father knew that was not fair to your mother."

"Your stepmother was not like your real mother. For one thing, she was a big and heavy woman, and another thing, I never once saw her smile."

"But, Anisan, you have to understand the situation at that time. It wasn't easy for her. When she got married to my father, she was a widow with four very young children. It wasn't easy to raise so many children with so little money. I know she worked as hard as my real mother."

"You are nice to say that about your stepmother. But, whatever you say, what I remember most about your stepmother was the beatings she gave you." Lefty looked grim and nodded his head. "Once when you and I were playing outside, she called you to help her with something. You didn't go in as quickly as she wanted, and so she grabbed the bamboo fishing pole that was leaning against the wall and she whacked you with the pole. She didn't stop, she whacked you and whacked you. You didn't flinch at all, and you didn't cry. I know it was painful. I felt so bad for you. To tell you the truth, your stepmother scared me."

"She scared me too. As a young boy I wondered why she would beat me so much and never my stepbrothers and stepsisters. I asked my father about it and he didn't say a word. He just looked away."

"You left home early to go to work, didn't you, Lefty? I bet it was because of your stepmother?"

"Well, I cannot lie. It was partly my stepmother and partly because there were so many mouths to feed. My father couldn't keep up. We were barely surviving financially. Of course, we weren't the only ones. In those early plantation days, many families struggled. When I became fifteen years old, my father said it was about time I went out to work to earn a living to help support the family. He told me to live away from home with the Filipino bachelors, and I did. I was so lonesome. You don't know how lonesome I was. There were many times I wanted to go home again. In fact, after a few days, did you know that I headed home? My father saw me walking down the road toward my home and he came running out. I was real, real happy because I thought he was going to welcome me home. I was so happy to see him. But I was wrong. He stopped me by the side of the road and said it was best that I never came home again, unless there was an emergency. It made me sad to hear my father said that. He told me that he couldn't help me. He told me to grow up to be a good man and never bring shame to the family. He told me to do the best I can in everything I do and by doing so, without fail I would succeed in whatever I set my heart on. Then, he put his hand in his pants pocket and took out a dollar and gently put it in my hands. A dollar in those days was worth a lot of money. He held my hands with a strong grip and said softly, 'Whatever may happen in the future, don't be bitter. Always be grateful.'"

"You never went back to Pāhoa after that, did you?"

"Only once, when I was seventeen, when my father died. He died very young, only about thirty-six years old."

"Do you have a grudge against your stepmother, Lefty?"

"At one time, I was angry at her. I could not forget all the beatings she gave me. As a young boy, when I was hurt and humiliated, I said to myself, 'Someday, I'm going to get my revenge and make you suffer.' But as the years went by, I would remember what my father had said, and I didn't want to be bitter all my life. Slowly, in my own mind, I think I began to understand her. I think she had no choice at that time. I probably needed discipline. Just scolding me might not be enough, because I may not have listened to her. After all, I had not accepted her as my mother. She wanted me to turn out to be a good person. No question, she was strict with me, and maybe really hard on me, but it was for my own good."

If our story were to end here, we would have been happy for Lefty that everything had turned out fine for him, but it was not to be.

One night, it was past nine o'clock when the telephone rang. My mother never liked having the telephone ring late at night. She said late calls, like telegrams, were inevitably bad news.

My father answered. It was Lefty. We could hear my father say, "What! When did that happen?" Then, a long silence; apparently Lefty was explaining what had happened. My father would grunt, "Uhm, uhm, hmmmmm."

Then, my father said to him, "Lefty, you are too emotional right now. Why don't you bring the kids and come over to our house. Let's talk about it here."

After my father hung up, my mother asked, "What happened to Lefty, Daddy?"

"It's his wife, Betty."

"Is she sick?"

"Sick in the head," replied my father.

"What do you mean?"

"She ran off with another man," muttered my father.

"Oh, my goodness," said my mother. "How sad for the children. How could she do that?"

That's exactly what I thought. How could a mother abandon her children and her husband? I assumed that a mother's love for her children was the strongest bond in nature. Even animals did not abandon their offspring.

In about half an hour, Lefty arrived with the two crying children. I remember the radio was on. "The Tennessee Waltz" was playing. My mother told me, "Roy, this is no time for music. Turn it off." Lefty was not in any condition to talk. I don't know whether he was angry at Betty or sorry that she had left him. Whatever it was, he was shaking uncontrollably.

Next day, Lefty's neighbor, Mrs. Santos, who knew the whole story from start to finish, explained to my mother, "And so, Lefty went to your house last night, huh? Well you know the story about Betty, huh?" Actually, my mother did not. "Anyway, you know Betty. She loves the good life, never cared for working or taking care of the children. I always tell her, 'Betty, you are one lucky woman. You have a wonderful husband. He works hard. He loves you and he takes good care of you. Show some appreciation. Clean the house sometimes. Don't let him do it all the time. Have the food ready when he comes home from work. He works all day. Let *him* rest when he comes home. You are terrible. Lefty is so nice to you. He does everything for you. You are treated like a queen.' Anyway, this musician comes with a band from Honolulu to play at the hotel. Betty goes dancing with her girlfriends. You know Lefty. He's the homebody type, doesn't care to go dancing. Well, to make a long story short, she sees the musician and the musician sees her. The people who went dancing tell me he is one good-looking man. Not short and skinny like Lefty. The musician—his name is Gilbert, I think—is tall, wavy hair, slick mustache, nice manners, real smooth operator. With a Clark Gable smile. You know, a little wicked. He plays the trumpet. He can sure blow that horn, I hear. He also sings with the band. Voice like honey syrup. Makes your knees weak when he gets up and sings. I guess Betty couldn't help it. She falls in love with this Gilbert guy. After the first night, she goes dancing alone so that she can see him. And Lefty? He let her go without complaining one bit. He tells her she's entitled to have some fun. What a nice guy, huh? You think my husband would say that to me? Holy Maria, Mother of Jesus, of course not. So, you know Betty. She goes night after night. That Gilbert guy, he's no dummy. He knows Betty is crazy about him. So, after he's through work, he and Betty go watch submarines. You know what I mean, eh, Mrs. Kodani?"

My mother managed to say, "I think I know what you mean, Mrs. Santos."

"To continue what I was saying. So, the other day, she's out all night and she comes back to the house yesterday morning. Lefty is up feeding the kids. 'What kind of woman is she?' I ask myself. Then, I begin to hear her yelling, 'I love Gilbert. Gilbert says he loves me. I'm sick and tired of living in this crummy town. No excitement. No nothing. You can have the kids. I just want out. I'm going with Gilbert to Honolulu. He says he's going to take good care of me. We're going to have a good life.' Then, I hear Lefty say, 'Betty, think about the children. They're young.'"

Years passed, and one night Betty telephoned Lefty from Honolulu. She said, "Lefty, I am very sorry, but I want to come back to you."

"Daddy, after what she did to us, she wants to come back?" Doris, the daughter, asked. Doris told Mrs. Santos, "My mother telephoned my father the other day after over twenty years and she says she is awfully sorry but she wants to come home to him. I told my father, no way. Let her stay in Honolulu. She hurt us so much, I still have pain and bad memories. I didn't want her back. I told him we were all happy without her, and if she came back, she would be nothing but trouble for us. My father, he's such a nice man. He tells me that he cannot refuse her. After all, she is still his wife and she is still our mother."

There was a reason for Betty returning to Lefty. She had a stroke and was partially paralyzed. In time, she became bedridden and had to be helped with even the smallest of daily functions.

Mrs. Santos would come by the store and give periodic reports to my mother, "Oh, Lefty is such a kind man. He is taking good care of Betty. You know, Lefty has to do everything for her now. She cannot do nothing, absolutely nothing anymore, completely helpless. She cannot speak—thank god for that—so you can't understand what she's trying to say. She tries, but because you cannot understand her, she becomes frustrated. But, Lefty is so patient. He feeds her and bathes her and everything else. He comes home at lunchtime to feed her. Doris comes around now and then, but you have to understand how she feels. She has a lot of hurt, and she and her brother cannot forgive her."

This went on for a few years. Lefty took care of his wife without ever complaining. He never asked anyone to help. He once told my father, "Anisan, if I became sick and needed help, I'm sure Betty would do the same for me." I don't know if Lefty was naïve or had lost his senses. Anyhow, Betty finally died, and Lefty took care of her at home to the end. He felt that she could not get the same kind of care at the hospital.

At the funeral, I would have thought that after carrying such a burden all these years Lefty would have felt a great sense of relief, but it was to be otherwise. He cried his heart out. He could not be consoled. His grief for his wife was simply overwhelming.

After the funeral, my mother said to us, "I felt more sorry for Lefty than for Betty. Even after what she had done to him, he took her back without saying anything. He took her back with open arms when she was sick and was of no use to him. He took care of her lovingly. He was willing to forget and forgive her. Lefty is a big-hearted man. There aren't too many people like him."

A few days later my father paid Lefty a visit to see whether everything was all right with him.

Lefty said to my father, "Anisan, you must think I'm crazy, and I cannot explain why I loved Betty so much but I loved her to the end. Even though she had left us, in a way I think I could kind of understand her reason for leaving. I know I'm not an exciting kind of guy. Even if I tried. When I found out that she was willing to marry me, I thought I was the luckiest guy on earth. So full of fun, so lively. So gorgeous too. On our wedding night, I couldn't believe how beautiful she was. After that, she could have anything she wanted from me. When she came back, to tell you the truth, I was so happy. Taking care of her was not a burden. In fact, I was glad to take care of her, especially since I knew she needed someone to take care of her. Finally, she needed me." ◆

DINNER
AT SIX

As high school classmates do, some of us had gathered in one of the hotel rooms after the formal reunion dinner had concluded to reminisce and talk story. At such gatherings, the usual matters of interest are classmates who have died, who are ill and those who are facing some kind of difficulty.

Then someone asked, "Hey, anybody know what happened to Dougie Boy (not his real name)? You were good friends with Dougie Boy, Roy. Do you know what happened to him?"

Except for money, Dougie Boy had everything going for him and he was a natural in everything he did. He was a leader of the guys. He was a born athlete and played well in basketball and baseball...coordinated, smooth and talented. And of course, he was tall, handsome and a crooner of songs like Frankie Avalon and a smooth dancer at a time when partners held each other close. All the girls loved him, but the love of his life was Rachel (not her real name), who was two years younger than we were. She was one of the prettiest girls in our high school; fortunate to have the genes of her mother, fair complexion with a cheerful disposition, and the genes of her father, smart with a radiant personality. I know other boys really liked Rachel, but Dougie Boy was the love of her life. During recess in our high school years, Dougie Boy and Rachel could always be seen together quietly chatting and holding hands. It seemed they had the world in their palms and the sun seemed to shine upon them with all the heavenly blessings.

During his senior year, Dougie Boy quit all his athletic activities without any explanation. I saw him working after school at one of the supermarkets as a bag boy, and he told me, "I have to work to earn my own money, Roy. I wanna go to the senior prom, and I have to rent a tux and buy a corsage for Rachel. Cost money. My father said go to work if I want to go to the prom."

The summer after graduation, I used to see Rachel waiting outside the supermarket where Dougie worked. Even in a small town like Hilo, you could always find a place for some privacy. When September approached, Dougie attended a small college in California to study engineering. During one of the summer college breaks, I returned home to Hilo and bumped into him eating a hamburger alone at the Dairy Queen on Waianuenue Avenue. He saw me first and called out, "Hey, Roy, howzit?"

I walked over to him, "Howzit, Dougie, what you doing?"

"I had to come home."

I immediately thought about Rachel.

"Nah, not what you think. Rachel is OK. I ran out of money and I cannot continue college. I gotta join the Army. My old man cannot help me anymore. You lucky your father helping you."

"Maybe after your military service, you can go back to college and finish up on the GI Bill."

"Yeah, I wanna do that. Rachel wants me to get a degree, and after that we going to get married. She said she gonna wait for me. How nice, yeah? You know me, Roy, I always wanted to get married to Rachel. There's nobody else for me. Even when I was in college in California, there were lots of good-looking women, but I know Rachel has a good heart and she will always be there when I need someone."

That was the last time I saw Dougie. I heard about him through the grapevine from other classmates. He did join the Army and after training camp he was sent to Germany. The next thing I heard about Dougie really surprised me. I heard that he married a German woman who worked in a beer garden near the military post. What! Dougie told me he was going to marry Rachel. I will never really know whether he truly loved the woman, but knowing Dougie, he's a friendly, gregarious guy. He must have been lonely without any close friends in Germany. Loneliness causes people to do things they would not ordinarily do, if they were not lonely. I felt sorry for Dougie, and I also felt sad for Rachel.

While in Honolulu, I used to visit my parents often in Hilo to pound *mochi* (glutinous rice) in late December. One late Saturday afternoon I was in the KTA Store on Keawe Street when I could feel someone staring at me. I waited awhile thinking it was just my imagination, when a woman approached me. It was Rachel.

"Hello, Roy. How are you?"

Before I could answer, Rachel started talking, and as she talked, it was like the waterfalls, she could not stop. "Do you know Dougie got married?"

Again, she didn't give me a chance to answer. "Dougie did not let me know personally. He sent his cousin to tell me that he got married and that he was sorry he could not keep his promise to marry me. I couldn't believe it. I thought our love for each other was so strong that nothing could tear us apart. Nothing. But, I was wrong. I cried and cried for weeks, maybe months. I lost weight, and I had to take a sick leave for six months. But, I realized there was nothing I could do, and I got married to a really understanding man from Kona. My husband is a school teacher like me. My husband is good to me, and I have nothing to complain about."

That was the last time I saw Rachel, but I heard several years later that her husband had cancer, and Rachel cared for him at home for about three of four years. He died, leaving a young son.

The years passed and one of my classmates who had made the Army his career was on the same flight to Hilo. It was he who mentioned to me that Dougie was now residing in Georgia with his three children. He had retired after twenty years of military service and was now working as a civilian in the officers' club on base. Dougie had divorced his wife, and she had returned to Germany.

Then out of the blue, I received a telephone call at my office from Dougie, "Hey, Roy, I'm at the airport. I'm going to Hilo for a family matter I have to take care. You know what? I called Rachel from Georgia last week and we're going to have dinner tomorrow night. What you think about that? Her husband died, and I'm free now because I divorced my wife. Maybe we can start all over again. We're not high school kids, and I think I'm wiser now."

I asked him to call me on his return flight to Georgia so that we could get together, but he said he was flying back from Kona and he promised to call me again when he was in Honolulu.

One of the women in my high school class told me later, "Roy, Rachel was so happy to hear from Dougie Boy. She couldn't believe she would see him again after all these years. She was like a teenager. She could not decide what dress to wear to their dinner, and so she went out to buy a new dress. At the same time she bought new shoes and a new bag. She got her hair and nails done. She didn't have much time, but she went to the health club and exercised every morning. She even bought sexy underwear, because she said it made her feel good. That's how excited she was."

Hilo is a small place. After Dougie arrived in Hilo and was walking along Kamehameha Avenue, he happened to catch a glimpse of Rachel without her knowledge. She was still very pretty and youthful, but at that moment he suddenly realized that too much water had flowed under the bridge, that he had traveled on many roads while she had continued to live in Hilo, that he was no longer the young high school student twenty-five years ago, that Georgia was now his home and he would not return to Hilo, that he had three children, that it would be unfair to ask Rachel to consider moving to Georgia away from Hilo where she had spent all her life, that to re-establish their relationship would be based on youthful dreams no longer real. Today was a different world from the one they knew in high school.

And so, he telephoned Rachel, "Rachel, I am very sorry but I have to cancel our dinner tomorrow night. I must return to Georgia right away."

As to be expected, there was a stunned silence, and then, "Why did you have to come back? You don't know how happy I was to hear from you last week. I could hardly sleep thinking I would see you again."

"Rachel, I will come to Hilo again. At that time, I promise to spend all my time with you. That's a promise."

"I think I can understand if we cannot have dinner tomorrow, but how about today. Just a few minutes today? That's all I will ever ask you again, just a few minutes. I want to see you, Dougie."

"I have to do some things, and so, I cannot see you today."

"Dougie, do you know how much I thought about you all these years. Even when my husband held me in his arms, I used to imagine it was you. It was so unfair to my husband. When I heard from you again, it was like a dream come true. I felt like a bird flying high in the sky, and now... Just a few minutes, Dougie, please. Don't make me feel so low. I'm begging you."

"I really promise to spend all my time with you the next time."

"Now, I wish you had not even called me last week. I will be a nervous wreck again. I don't think I can take this. I'm so disappointed at you again. You are so insensitive."

"I will make it up to you the next time, Rachel. I want you to be happy."

"Happy? I am so miserable."

Dougie heard Rachel sobbing and then heaving over the telephone. Then, he heard the telephone click. ◆

FOR BETTER OR FOR WORSE

Several years ago when I returned to Hilo for a family memorial service, I happened to see Mr. and Mrs. Kato (a fictitious name for this story), who were walking on the *mauka* (mountain) side of Kilauea Street near Hilo Hongwanji temple. Mrs. Kato, a small, thin woman, about ninety pounds, wearing a dark granny dress, was holding her husband's hand and leading him as he walked slowly and haltingly with his right hand curled to his side. Later someone told me that he had a stroke and could only speak in grunts.

Mr. Kato, who must have weighed about 200 pounds or more, had been a carpenter. My parents knew both Mr. and Mrs. Kato well. Mrs. Kato and my mother were good friends, because they both liked ornamental plants and flowers. The Katos had two daughters several years older than I. Both of them eventually became public school teachers in Honolulu.

When I was young, maybe about four or five years old, I used to go to their house and I would wait until the daughters returned from school. They often used to buy me candy or gum from Haili Store on the way home from school. I still remember the time they invited me to dinner and made cucumber and mayonnaise sandwiches. I thought it was the greatest sandwich in the world at that time, and after dinner I ran home and told my mother to make me cucumber and mayonnaise sandwiches. My mother made it once, but my father said it was a *haole* (Caucasian) sandwich, which was not enough to fill him up. We never had it after that.

Mr. Kato was always nice to me. It could be that I was the son he never had. He once asked me, "Shun-chan, you wanna fly a kite?" Of course, I wanted to fly a kite, and so he got some bamboo and some old newspapers, and he made a kite. He did not use glue or paste to hold the newspaper to the bamboo sticks. He went into the kitchen and used leftover rice to bind the newspaper to the sticks. Then, we walked over to Mo'oheau Park. I still remember how happy I was to fly the kite, and so, I ran with the kite trailing me. But, Mr. Kato smiled and said, "Shun-chan, no need run. Just let the wind fly the kite." He stood in the middle of the park. This was a time when there were still buildings on the ocean side of Kamehameha Avenue. He was right. Suddenly, the wind from the ocean caught the kite and carried it inland where the fish market used to be on the corner of Kamehameha Avenue and Mamo Street. Then, as the kite was flying high above us, he passed the string to me. To a young boy there is no greater pleasure than to hold a kite soaring in the sky and to watch it swooping in arcs this way and that way. It is a freedom of sheer pleasure.

Nice as he was to me, there was another side to Mr. Kato. A dark side that caused tremendous fear in me. When Mr. Kato used to drink beer, he literally turned into a monster, and lost his composure. He would be abusive to his wife. There used to be nails in bags near the kitchen, and he would throw the nails at Mrs. Kato and shout at her, "*Baka* (crazy)! Baka!" He would continue this barrage of senseless words in Japanese. His daughters would shout, "Otosan, *yamete* (stop it). Yamete." He would not stop. On a really bad day, he would strike Mrs. Kato in her face. I know all the neighbors could hear the shouting and the yelling, and the painful cries of Mrs. Kato. In those days, no one called the police. No one intruded. This was a family matter to be handled within the family. My parents knew about it and my mother would merely say, "*Kawaiso* (poor thing)."

Whenever Mr. Kato began to strike his wife, I would be so scared that I would flee home, and I would be shaking. My parents would calm me down by opening a bottle of soda pop and handing the bottle to me to drink.

Years later I used to wonder if Mr. Kato was an alcoholic, or whether he drank when he was frustrated, or maybe both. I still do not know why men are so abusive to their wives or girlfriends. Sometimes, now when I read the newspaper, it seems that the man is jealous or feels inadequate or his male pride is hurt. I don't believe Mr. Kato could have been jealous about his wife, a small, thin woman, but who knows? Maybe he was.

My mother used to tell me that Mr. Kato was still abusive to his wife, even as he got older. For some reason, Mrs. Kato never divorced

her husband. Maybe it was her Japanese upbringing of that generation, when many second-generation Japanese-Americans did not
divorce, even if the woman suffered physical and mental pain. The older
Japanese used to say, "*Gaman* (persevere)."

Then, Mr. Kato suffered a stroke. Fortunately for him, he was not
bedridden, but his right side was paralyzed and he could not speak.
Because it was hard to understand him, he began to shout. My mother
told me, "Mrs. Kato is so shame her husband is shouting all the time
and the neighbors can hear him. They going to move to her brother's
house on Piopio Street, because her brother has a house with a base-
ment that might help so that no can hear him shouting."

In 1960 there was a tidal wave that destroyed a major part of Hilo,
including Waiākea Town, the remaining buildings along Kamehameha
Avenue, and most of the houses on Piopio Street. The night the tidal
wave struck Hilo, the electricity went out in downtown Hilo. As the
waves poured in destructive force, Mrs. Kato scrambled to help her
husband escape to higher ground toward Kilauea Avenue. Her brother
told her, "*Nesan* (older sister), just run away. Save your life." It took a
tremendous effort on her part to hold Mr. Kato tightly as they tried
to run away from the incoming waves. It was dark and the waters
were rising. People were shouting. The debris from the waves was pil-
ing high. Mr. Kato thought his wife would abandon him, and so he
cried incoherently, "Ah! Ah! Ah!" My mother said she doesn't how Mrs.
Kato did it, but she carried her husband on her back, *opa* style, and
dragged him in the rising water to Kilauea Avenue. Even with years of
abuse, Mrs. Kato did not let go of her husband. She herself could have
drowned that night, but she saved him. Why she did, no one knows.

After the tidal wave, I understand Mr. Kato no longer shouted at
his wife, but as he grew older, he had to rely more and more on his
wife for everything. I do not know whether Mrs. Kato did everything
for her husband, because it was her duty to gaman and take care of
husband, or whether it was some kind of love for her husband. And if
it was not love, then maybe it was some kind of psychological, incom-

prehensible understanding that many women have for their spouses that men will never know or understand. ◊

THE DOGS
OF WAR

In war, the best and the worst of people are obvious. There are heroes such as the *nisei* (second-generation) young men who volunteered as soldiers and fought during World War II serving in Europe and Asia. They served with distinction and received high military medals for their heroism. Then there are people in the Japanese-American community in Hawai'i who were scoundrels.

One afternoon in the mid-1960s, my father and two of his friends were chatting at my father's hardware store in Hilo when a male customer walked in. One of the friends looked up and whispered, "Goddamn *inu*."

After the customer and the friends left the store, I asked my father, "What is an inu? Isn't inu the Japanese word for dog?"

He answered, "As you know, all of the *nikkeijin* (Americans of Japanese ancestry) in Hawai'i were loyal to America. There were no known spies or people who were disloyal to America, but there were nikkeijin in Hawai'i who reported to the FBI that some of the nikkeijin were not to be trusted, that they were disloyal to America. These people who secretly reported others were called inu."

"How did people know who the inu were?"

"Hawai'i is a small place. There is no secret in Hawai'i. Somehow, people knew about other people and what people do."

I asked, "Do you know who the inu in Hilo were?"

"Of course, everybody knew the inu."

"Who were the inu in Hilo?"

I was shocked. One of the names he disclosed was a close family friend of ours. I could not believe it.

Later, one of my good friends in Honolulu, Paul, an architect, told me that his family had been sent to one of the relocation camps on the Mainland. His father was a congregational minister on Kaua'i at that time. He was a highly regarded community leader. Most of the men and their families who were sent to the Mainland camps were Buddhist and Shinto priests, others were Japanese language school teachers and still others were prominent business leaders. Paul's father was a Christian minister. Many of the leaders on Kaua'i requested the FBI not to send Paul's father and the family to the internment camp, but the request was denied for some unknown reason. Even today they still do not know who the inu was.

I asked my father, "Dad, why did the inu report others when they knew that they were giving false information?"

"Many inu reported others to get on the good side of the FBI. By reporting others, they thought this would show their loyalty to America. It didn't matter if the information was not true. They were terrible people, but what could we do? If we complained to the FBI, the FBI would think we were disloyal. War brings out the worst in people. In bad times, you don't know who to trust. People say that some of the inu in Honolulu were prominent leaders of the Japanese-American community." ◆

MY DREAM BICYCLE

Tommy was the first to get a bicycle in the neighborhood. Being the youngest in his family, his mother gave him whatever he wanted. He was never denied anything. He wanted a Schwinn bicycle and he got a Schwinn bicycle for his tenth birthday, which fell in January. I had never forgotten his birthday because he always got his birthday presents before I did—my birthday was in February.

Then, Nicky got a shining blue Schwinn bicycle a few weeks later. Bobby got a Schwinn bicycle with a little horn attached to the handlebars that made a loud toot when he grasped the black bulb. Soon, thereafter, Lloyd and Corky get Schwinn bicycles. It seemed all the boys in the neighborhood got a bicycle. All they had to do was to ask their parents. If they had gotten what they wanted, I certainly could do the same.

One evening before my father came home from work, I went up to my mother as she was cooking and said, "Ma, you know my birthday is coming soon, huh, Ma?"

"Yes, I know, Roy. It's next week?"

"Do you know what I really would like for my birthday this year?"

"I have a pretty good idea what you would like, Roy, but why don't you tell me, because I could be wrong."

"I really would like a bicycle. A Schwinn bicycle. A silver one with a mirror on the handlebar so that I can see the rear as I'm riding around. That's what I would like for my birthday."

"Roy, that's what I thought you would like for your birthday."

"Then, can I have a bike?"

My mother turned around and looked at me and said nothing at first. She was not smiling. She stood there looking at me. "You cannot have a bicycle, Roy."

I was flabbergasted. Astounded. I couldn't believe it. Did I hear her correctly? All the boys in the neighborhood had a bike. Why not me? It didn't make sense. I asked, "Why not, Ma? Why not?"

"Daddy has just started a new business. He's opened a new hardware store. We had to borrow money to put up the building and to open the store. You are old enough now, and so, I am going to tell you, Daddy had to borrow money from the bank. He also borrowed money from your uncles and aunties and some of his friends. A bicycle is a luxury and we cannot afford any luxury right now. We must pay off all our loans before we can afford any luxury. It just wouldn't look right if you were riding a nice shining new bicycle when we have not paid off our loans. Your uncles and aunties would wonder what kind of people we are, buying you a bicycle without paying back their money. The right thing to do is to pay back all the loans first. Buying necessities is understandable but not a bicycle, which is expensive. That, they would never tolerate. They might even ask Daddy to pay off their loans immediately if they were to see you riding around with a new bike. Roy, we don't have the money to repay everyone's loan right now. Now, do you understand why you cannot have a new bike for your birthday?"

To be very honest, at that age, I couldn't quite understand what she was talking about. All I knew was that all the boys had a bike and I wanted one very badly. It was as simple as that. I felt like crying. I was also upset at my father for opening a new store and denying me the silver bicycle I really, really wanted. Without a new store, I could have had a new bicycle. He could have continued to work as an employee of the farmers cooperative where he had worked for many years. Why couldn't he have continued? Why couldn't he have been satisfied with his old job?

Down deep inside I had false hope. I prayed that my parents would relent and buy the bike I dreamt about.

A few days before my birthday I approached my mother with a compromise. "Ma, about that bike."

"Yes, what about it, Roy?"

"It doesn't have to be a Schwinn bike, Ma. It can be any bike, as long as it is a bike. Any color is OK and I don't need any accessories."

"Roy, I told you. You cannot have a bicycle. You just cannot have a bike. I want you to give up the idea of getting a bike for your birthday.

For that matter, you won't be able to get a bike for a very long time as long as we have loans to pay. You must understand that."

I did not give up. I prayed fervently. God would not disappoint me. I had been good. In fact, I promised to be good for the rest of my life if He would only grant me this one wish. For sure, with my solemn promise for good behavior, God would look favorably upon me. I was sure God would understand my feelings.

On the morning of my birthday, I jumped out of bed and ran to the living room. There was no bike there. I ran from one room to the other, this way and that way. No bike anywhere. I dashed outside looking for my bike. No bike at all. I rushed into the house. My father and mother were in the kitchen having breakfast. Neither of them spoke at first. My father then said, "Come here, Roy. Mama and I wanted to give you a bike for your birthday. All parents want to see their children happy. We know you would have been happy to get a bike for your birthday. But, Mama already told you why we cannot give you a bike. I want you to be a man. You cannot have everything you want in life. Sometimes, you must wait. Sometimes, what you want is far beyond our means. Sometimes, you must make sacrifices. A bicycle is not something you need for school. It is not something you are required to have. It is an expensive toy. There will be other things in your life more important than a bike that you will need. At that time, no matter how expensive it is, Mama and I will make whatever sacrifice we must make so that you can have those important things."

"What is more important than a bike, huh, Daddy?" I asked.

"Someday you may want to go to college, and at that time, even if I am having a hard time, I promise to pay for your college education."

"But, Daddy, I may not want to go to college. Why worry about college now? I got many, many years ahead of me before I can even think about college."

"I can't answer that, but I want you to know that I will do my best to send you to college, if and when you decide you want to go to college someday. College education is expensive, but we will do whatever we can for your education. That's all I'm saying to you now, so that you will know that when it comes to important things we will try to manage somehow to pay for those important things."

As it turned out, I did want to go to college. Hard as it was financially for my parents, they kept their promise, and I was able to go off to college in Pennsylvania. They made tremendous sacrifices to enable me to attend college. During my college years, I did work during the summers and waited on tables during the school year. Lafayette College, my alma mater, gave me a partial scholarship, but the bulk of the financial burden was upon my parents. They worked seven days a week, year in and year out. They never took a day off and never had a vacation until many years later when they retired from the business. After college, I wanted to go to law school, and at that time, there was no law school in Hawai'i. Without any hesitation, without question, my parents again paid for most of my tuition, books, room and board. Even while I was attending college and law school, the loans had not yet been paid in full. It was a financial struggle for my parents having to pay down the loan and at the same time, having to help me financially with my education.

When the loans were paid off, which were several years after I graduated my law school, my mother said, "I can now breathe easy. All these years, I felt as though I had a bag of rocks on my back. The yoke is finally off. I don't want ever to have to borrow money again."

I can never forget my tenth birthday because I was so disappointed. I pouted all day long. I was miserable for weeks. Just as I was disappointed with my parents, I was also disappointed with God. How could He have failed me? What more did I need to do to satisfy God so that He would grant me a simple wish? I could not understand God. Had I not promised Him that if He were to grant me my one wish I would be good for the rest of my life? That was a tough promise for anyone to make but I had made it. Yet, He had not come through for me. If He could not grant me a simple wish, how reliable was He? This was the first time I bargained with God, and it was not to be my last. Time after time in the future when I wanted something badly, very badly, I would make a solemn pact with God, promising to do something in return for my wish. But, as usual, my wishes were rarely granted. Still, I continued to bargain with God, hoping that my wish would be granted. I prayed fervently. All God heard from me was "Gimme, gimme." It dawned on me that God was not Santa Claus. Once at Kalaupapa on Moloka'i, a Roman Catholic priest said, "Because we are human, we try to negotiate with God, usually when we want something. You can negotiate with people, but the question is...can you negotiate with God?"

Sometimes, children can be mean. Intentionally or not, the boys would cruise by my home on their bikes and toot their horns. I died each time they went by. I never went out for about a month after my birthday because I could not stand to see the boys riding by. To make things worse, Gladys, one of the girls in the neighborhood got a bike too. She would ride her bike pass our home slowly, ever so slowly, and call out, "Roy!" I don't know if she was taunting me or just calling me. Whatever it was, I felt sick.

My parents were never able to buy me bike. Years later, while visiting one of my college classmates in Connecticut, he asked me, "Roy, would you like to go for a bike ride in the country?"

"That's a terrific idea. I would enjoy riding a bike," I answered.

"You can ride my brother's old bike," he said.

We walked to the garage and opened the door. At the far end in the shadow, leaning against the wall were two bicycles. One was an English bicycle, and of all things the other was a silver Schwinn bike, like the bicycle I had dreamt about. A little rusty but exactly what I had wanted.

"You mind riding my brother's old Schwinn bike?" asked my classmate.

"Heck, no. You don't know what it means to me," I replied.

"What do you mean?" he asked.

"It's too long to explain. Let's just ride," I said as I hopped on and rode out.

It was a pleasant enough bike ride, but it wasn't like riding on Kapiolani Street with the rest of the gang when everyone else had a bike. Disappointments die hard. ◆

THE LOVING
DAUGHTER

I could never tell whether she was an old woman or a young woman, or an old-looking young woman, or a young-looking old woman. She wore her hair in an old woman's bun and dressed in drab old woman's clothing. And whenever I saw her, she was always with an old man, her father, who we used to refer to as Sato-man.

As long as I could remember, Sato-man spoke roughly and brusquely to his daughter, Mi-chan. Sato-man was a farmer who would come to my father's hardware store to pick up fertilizer and supplies now and then. I never saw him smile. He always had a frown, like he was angry at the world. He would say with a sneer, "Hurry up and pay. Don't keep Kodani-san waiting for his money."

My father would tactfully reply, "That's all right. Take your time. You may find something else you need for your farm."

Sato-man would say, "Michiko, time is money. Don't waste time. If our business here is finished, let's move along. The sun doesn't stop in the middle of the sky just because you want to talk story. The sun keeps on moving along, you know."

Mi-chan and my mother had been classmates in school, and living on an isolated farm miles from town, Mi-chan must have looked forward to the occasional trips to town. Whenever she had a chance, she would snatch a minute or two to talk to my mother. The time she spent with my mother was like a tonic for her. After a few minutes of animated conversation with my mother, her eyes would light up and her pallid cheeks would take on a bright glow.

She would say to my mother, "Toyo-chan, you are very lucky. You have a nice husband and your children are healthy and they are well behaved. I don't know why I have this kind of life. I guess I must have been bad in my other life. I must suffer now for all my badness."

"Mi-chan, you shouldn't think like that. There is a reason for our condition. I am grateful for what I have and I think you should be too. It may not be the best for you now, but who knows, maybe in the future, it will suddenly turn for better. Don't look at the bad side. Look at the bright side of things, Mi-chan."

"But, for most of my life, I've had a hard time."

"How old were you when your mother died? It's been so long that I can't remember."

"I was about three or four years old at that time. Young as I was, I can still see my mother in bed. Her eyes were sunken in, hardly moving. Her lips were all cracked and dry like an old woman. Her skin was yellow, a sick yellow. More than an illness, when I think about it now, I think she died from exhaustion. She must have been too tired to go on. It would have been a little easier for my mother if my father had been just a little bit more understanding and kind. More patient. She had no time for herself. No time to rest. No time to relax. But, you know my father, he's always pushing from the time he gets up in the morning until he goes to bed. He was always demanding things be done right away and be done quickly. I think my poor mother finally   just gave up. Before her final breath, she held my hand gently and said, 'Michiko. *Shiawase* (happiness).' She had tears in her eyes. When my mother died, my father did not cry at all. He said crying was a sign of weakness. To this day, I have never seen my father cry."

Once Sato-man bought a ton of fertilizer and my father delivered the fertilizer to his farm and I tagged along with him. His farm was several miles from the main highway and we traveled on a dirt and cinder road through the sugarcane fields to get there. The elevation was high and the farm was close to the forest. At about six o'clock in the late afternoon, the air was nippy and cool. As we drove into the storage house, someone came out wearing boots, a long denim shirt, Levis and a pith helmet. I assumed it was Sato-man. It was not. It was Mi-chan.

From the opposite direction came Sato-man, similarly dressed. He ordered Mi-chan in a gruff voice, "Michiko, unload the fertilizer."

My father responded, "No. I'll unload the fertilizer myself. It's nothing for me. I can do it myself. In fact, it's easier if I do it myself."

"Michiko, I said to help Kodani-san. Hurry up. Don't just stand there watching."

Mi-chan seized a bag of fertilizer, each weighing 100 pounds and swung it on her shoulders and walked to the storage house. My father carried five bags and Mi-chan carried the other five bags. It was then that I realized that Mi-chan was doing man's work on her father's farm. She may not have done all of the work, but she was certainly doing a great portion of the work.

Sato-man took a great liking to me and he would advise me like a favorite nephew. "Kodani-boy, remember, a man cannot be weak. Don't be a sissy. Don't be afraid of anybody, no matter his size. It's what's inside that counts, not how big you are. If anybody wants to act tough, take 'em on. Fight 'em! Fight 'em to the end. Don't give up! The more you fight, the more people respect you. You understand?"

I said I understood. I don't know if I agreed with him. My father, who was listening quietly on the side, would say later to me after we left Sato-man, "Roy, I'm sure there are times when you must fight. There may be no other choice but to fight. Yet, on the other hand, there may be times when you should not fight, or it might be foolish for you to fight. You must learn to know the difference."

My mother's opinion on the matter was consistent. "You don't have to fight to settle a problem. Why do men always talk about fighting? Fighting is for *yabanjin* (barbarians). Act civilized."

One mid-afternoon in July, when nothing was moving and the only sound that could be heard was the heavy moan of the engine of a car moving on the street, Sato-man drove up to the front of the store. Mi-chan bounced out and hurriedly walked in. She could hardly suppress a smile.

"Toyo-chan. Toyo-chan," she said to my mother. "Guess what?"

"What is it? Obviously, it must be something very good. You sound so happy. Tell me, what is the good news?"

"You know Yamamoto-san, who lives in the other camp? The one, you know, the wife died about a year ago?"

"Oh, yes, Yamamoto-san. He's a big man, but a gentle and kind-hearted person. He's a quiet man, but I think he's a very nice man. Yes, what about him?"

"Well, he's been coming around to our house recently. I didn't think much about it at first. After all, he's been a neighbor for a long time. He's about five or six years older than us. Well, the funny thing is, he has been bringing all kinds of vegetables and fruits when he visits us. I couldn't figure it out. Why all of a sudden? I just thought he was just nice to us."

"Hmmmm. It may be more than that, Mi-chan."

"I think so too. Last Sunday he came to our house after lunch when I washing clothes and he asked my father if he could take me riding. My father said it was up to me, but I had to finish my washing first. I was so surprised, I couldn't think straight. I got confused. He sat on the front steps until I finished. You know, Toyo-chan, I don't have any nice clothes. So, I looked in my mother's clothes chest and I found a dress my mother wore. It wasn't the best, but it was better than anything I have. We went riding. Yamamoto-san is a quiet man as you say, and I don't talk too much too, and so I didn't say too much. But, I had this feeling I never had before. Somehow, it felt good to know that there is somebody who kind of likes me. Do you know what I mean, Toyo-chan?"

"Oh, Mi-chan. I am so happy for you. Everybody needs somebody to love you and for you to love. This is natural. Love gives meaning to life. It makes you want to live, no matter how bad things may seem to be."

"Before he took me home, he stopped at the plantation store and bought me an ice cream cone. I felt like a young girl. It sounds crazy, but I felt like giggling and laughing. I was so happy. It wasn't the ice cream. It was knowing that he cared enough to spend money on me. It was the first time in my life anyone ever bought me anything. I wanted to cry because he was so nice."

"Oh, I'm glad to hear that."

"It felt so good knowing that I meant something to him."

"You must be someone special to Yamamoto-san."

"Do you really think so?"

"Mi-chan, I think he may ask you to marry him."

"I'm afraid of that. That means I would have to live with him and nobody will take care of my father."

"You have taken care of your father all these years. He is strong and healthy. He can take care of himself if he really wants to. He must let you go. You deserve some happiness. You have your life to live too. Yamamoto-san is a good man. I'm pretty sure he will make you happy. This is your chance, Mi-chan. In fact, your father should marry someone to take care of him."

"There is another thing. I have never told anyone, but since you have been my good friend all these years, I must tell you. I must tell someone before I go crazy keeping it a secret."

"My goodness. What is it?"

"From the time I was about thirteen or fourteen years old, I was like a wife to my father. Do you know what I'm trying to say? My father never got remarried. In a way, I wish he had. You know men have to have—Toyo-chan, you know what I'm trying to say?"

"Yes. You don't have to say anymore, I understand. But, whatever happened in the past, forget about it and go on with life. That's the best thing to do. Think about the future."

Yamamoto-san did ask Mi-chan to marry him.

"Mi-chan, I am not a rich man, but what little I have, I am willing to share with you. I am not exactly a young man, but at the same time I promise to do whatever I can to make you happy. I want you to marry me. You are a very sincere person. You are honest. You work hard. When you smile, I feel like smiling too. I like to be near you, and when you're not around, I miss you very much."

"Yamamoto-san, thank you very, very much for asking me. I am so happy. You don't know how happy you've made me. But, first, I have to ask my father."

"Yes, I know. Your father is getting old. He can come and live with us if he wants to."

Mi-chan was thrilled. She was deliriously overjoyed. She promptly told her father about it.

"What! Yamamoto asked you to what?"

"To marry him."

"No! No! No! No!"

"Why, Papa, why?"

"Who's going to take care of me?"

"Yamamoto-san said you could come to live with us, if you want to."

"How about this farm, huh? Did you think about this farm? We put in a lot of hard work on this farm? Years and years of hard work, day in and day out. And now, you want me to give it up and go to live with you on Yamamoto's farm? No! I won't go to live with him. I stay here. If you wanna marry him, go ahead, but don't ever come back because I don't want to see somebody who is not grateful for everything I do for you. You understand?"

Mi-chan cried her heart out. She knew Yamamoto-san's proposal would be the first and last, and to decline it would be unbearable, but she did.

Yamamoto-san asked, "Is there something about me you don't like?"

"No. You are the nicest man I have ever met and I know I would be happy and proud to be your wife, but—"

"But what?"

"It's my father. I have to take care of him. He doesn't want to leave the farm."

Mi-chan sacrificed a life she could have had with Yamamoto-san to remain with her father. From that day on, she aged even faster.

Several months later, my mother learned that Yamamoto-san married a widow, a woman considerably older than he. It may not have been love, but in his loneliness, he sought companionship.

A year or so later, her father had a severe stroke on his right side. Sato-man now had to depend on Mi-chan for everything. He was completely helpless. Mi-chan had to do all the work on the farm. She would bring her father to town now and then. The right side of his face sagged, and when he spoke, he sputtered and grunted. It was difficult to understand him. Yet, he continued to holler at her unintelligibly. Mi-chan obediently did what he wanted without saying a word. Her hair turned gray and she began walking with a stoop. Caring for her father was taking a terrible toll on her. The strain was getting too much for her.

My mother asked her, "Mi-chan, is there anybody in the family who can help you take care of your father? You need some rest sometimes."

"I cannot ask anyone to help me. My father has to be taken care in a certain way. Only I know what to do. He gets upset when I even leave him for a minute. If his condition gets worse, he may get another stroke, and so I try to be there by his side and try not to get him too excited."

About a year later, Sato-man had another stroke and a cerebral hemorrhage, and he died. It is not nice to say this, but his death was a reprieve for Mi-chan. If he had lingered on, my mother felt Mi-chan would have died before him from stress and aggravation.

I understand only a few people attended his funeral. His relatives made an obligatory appearance. Only my parents could be counted as friends.

After the funeral, my mother approached Mi-chan and asked her, "Is there anything I can do for you? You are now all alone."

"Thank you very, very much, Toyo-chan. I appreciate everything you and your husband did for me. You may think it is strange, but no matter how hard my father was, I could never hate him. Already, I kind of miss him, and already I am feeling very sad for him."

"I know it will take time, but you must go on. Maybe things will get better for you."

"Toyo-chan, do you know that to the very end my father was bitter? I tried my very best to make him happy, but he was never happy with me. He was never satisfied with the way I did things for him. I tried and I tried. He never forgave my mother."

"What are you talking about?"

"My father wanted a son. He scolded my mother from the day I was born to the day she died that she should have given birth to a son. What could she do? To make it up to him, I tried to do everything possible to be like a son to him, but he never accepted me. Never. He had wanted a son so badly, nothing else mattered to him. He was blind to everything I did for him. Knowing that I was not wanted was a terrible feeling. It made me feel very low. Yet, I loved my father, but he never once showed me any affection. When he spoke to me, even as a child, his voice was harsh. He always had a disgusted look. I could take the yelling, the coldness and the mistreatment. If he had only shown a little affection, that he cared, just a little. It would have made up for everything, but he never did. And that hurt me the most. I guess with all the years of bitterness, he never could."

As my parents drove away from the cemetery, in a remote corner of a high pasture in the fading light of the day, my mother turned to look to be sure that Mi-chan was all right. Everyone was gone by then. Mi-chan could be seen arranging what few flowers there were on the freshly covered grave, and then she stood and with her head bowed, she clasped her hands together in silent prayer for the peaceful repose of her father's soul, who while living had been restless and tormented. Always, always, Mi-chan was the loving and devoted daughter, who sacrificed so much of her own happiness to gain so little from her father. ◆

FROM DREAMS
TO ASHES

First was the odor—overpowering, coming suddenly out of nowhere; caustic, acrid, heavy and threatening. It was unmistakably the odor of a hostile fire. The irritating, sulfurous smell cut sharply through the early autumn evening. We all sniffed the ominous air, trying to detect where the smell was coming from. There is nothing like a hostile fire to cause you worry and anxiety because it is always destructive. It destroys your possessions, your accumulations and with that a part of your life is gone forever.

There were still remnants of the day as we all looked out the window. The western sky was aglow with bright colors painted with hues of red, orange, yellow, violet against the fading pale blue background. We were preparing for dinner. A time when our family all got together and talked about the day's events. Mama prepared simple meals. This was long before the medical concern for nutrition, diet and cholesterol. Mama used common sense in preparing a balanced meal. Rice was the staple. Plenty of vegetables, usually with fish, meat or pork. Chicken was not as common as it is today. Chicken then was served on auspicious occasions or at parties. Chicken hekka, cooked in soy sauce with burdocks, tofu, green onions and long rice was usually prepared at parties by my father. It was a male thing like hamburgers over the grill outdoors.

At dusk, the mynah birds in the mango tree across the street would be usually squawking in a riotous cacophony of chirping and chattering before settling down for the evening. Not today. There was an eerie, foreboding silence. When tragedy strikes, even the birds know.

Seconds later, a voice like a deadly dagger stabbing our hearts cried out in the neighborhood, "Fire! Fire! Fire!"

We ran out to our porch. There it was—the dark, black, sinister billowing smoke spiraling upward, casting a doom-like spell over everything it touched. Soon the smoke filled the vast sky with darkness. You always worry that the fire may not be contained and may rage out of control, burning your home.

"It's coming from the Seventh-day Adventist Church," hollered my father. "I must go and help."

As he ran toward the church, my brother and I followed close behind. I must confess that I was excited. Everyone was running toward the church. The adults intending to do whatever they could to help. A minute or two later, the wailing siren of the fire trucks racing up the hill was heard. You always wonder if the firemen will be able to save the home and rescue the occupants in time. No matter how soon they arrive, it is never soon enough in times of tragedy.

We approached the church expecting a great, big fire raging out of control, consuming the church. But, fortunately for the church, the disaster had struck elsewhere. The toolshed in the back of the church was on fire. It is difficult to measure a tragedy, and in this case, merely because it was a shed did not mean it was a lesser tragedy. It was an extremely sad one.

Those who didn't know would have simply scoffed and said that it was just a shed on fire and would have probably walked away with some relief, but the neighbors who knew the old Japanese man that lived in the shed felt sad and pity for him. He was hunched from years of toil. There he was, hysterical and screaming in Japanese, "I must get back in. I must get my tin box. I must! I must! Let me go. Please. Let me go back in. Oh, please, god! Please, god! I must go and get my box."

"No. No. You cannot go inside. Fire, too big. You might get hurt. Worse, you might die, if you go in," said one of the two firemen holding him back.

"Let me go. Let me go," the old man cried.

"You go, you die," the other fireman said sympathetically.

The old man strained to free himself. For some reason he had to retrieve the tin box. It seemed that life itself depended on that box which was now in the shed burning out of control. He wept and his sorrowful moaning was like a wounded man. He could no longer speak. He just groaned like an animal. I guess it was too much for him to bear to see the shed burning. He sat on the ground with his back to the fire. It was pathetic to see and hear him.

As quickly as it had started, the firemen were able to control the fire in a matter of minutes. By then, the old man was crying uncontrollably, his head bowed down. The minister's wife gently wrapped a blanket around his shoulders.

All that was left was the black skeleton of the burnt shed. We could hear the sizzling of some embers not yet out. Night had descended upon us and it was now dark and we could only see by the light of the streetlights across the way. The fire captain walked into what remained of the shed and groped in the ashes. He seemed to know what to look for. As an old timer, he had experienced enough tragedies to know what to look for without being told. I guess he had seen other heartaches in performing his job. With a stick, he searched in the ashes. As we watched, he pushed something with his iron-toe boots. It was a tin box the size of a loaf of bread.

The captain brought the tin box to the old man, who leaped forward when he saw the box. His hands shook badly like he had palsy.

"You want me to open it?" asked the captain softly.

"Yes. Yes," the old man answered.

The captain opened the box. We all leaned forward as a group to look. There was nothing in it, except ashes. Yes, only ashes. The high temperature of the fire had incinerated all of its contents and everything had disintegrated. The old man grabbed the box and with his right hand scooped out the ashes. His eyes round and wide with utter disbelief. He couldn't contain himself. He collapsed and beat the ground with his gnarled, bare hands. The only sound that came forth was an agonizing guttural, "Ahhhhhhhhhhhhhhhhhhhhhhhh!" It was a combination of frustration, sadness and deep emotional pain. At first, I wondered what the old man had kept in the tin box that was so important to him.

Then, he screamed out, "My money! My money! Ohhhh! Ohhhh! My money! My money! Ohhhh!"

It was then that I knew what it had contained. It had contained cash. The old man had probably not believed in banks and he had saved all of his earnings in the small tin box. Now, in a matter of seconds, all of his earnings were wiped out and there was nothing to show for all his years of hard work. Absolutely nothing.

We didn't know his name. No one seemed to know much about him. He was a bachelor who lived alone and apparently had no friends. The church in a gesture of Christian kindness and charity had permitted him to live in the shed.

The minister's wife told the neighbors, "He was the church gardener for many years. He had started long before my husband and I were assigned to this church. He tended to the yard once a week and a number of years ago he asked if he could leave all his personal things in the toolshed. Of course, we had no objection. Then, a year or two later, he came to us one evening after he had finished his day's work and asked if he could sleep in the shed. We thought surely he must be joking. But, he was never more serious. We told him it was not suitable to live in. It was just a toolshed, hardly enough room for the tools. No electricity, no water. 'Never mind,' he said. 'All I need is a place to sleep.' We suggested that if he didn't have any money that the state could assist him with some welfare money. 'No, no welfare money. Just let me live in shed,' he pleaded. What could we say? So, that's how he came to live in the tool shed.

"He worked as, what we referred to then as a 'yard man,' a gardener. He had no car and he would go to the homes of those who hired him by pushing his manual lawn mower. In the late afternoon, we would see him pushing his lawn mower home. He would always be talking to himself. I guess that's what happens when you live alone for so many years.

"Once I asked him, 'Why don't you enjoy life sometimes? You work so hard and you do nothing to enjoy life.' The old man answered, 'My family in Japan very poor. I come to Hawai'i very young man. I work hard in Hawai'i. No shame to work hard. I save all my money. I waste nothing. I save everything. Only spend money when I need. I eat enough to live. I wear simple clothes. No need have fancy clothes. No need car. I can walk. Someday I go back to my home in Japan. I can retire with my money I save. When I go back, I tell my family and my friends, 'My life in Hawai'i hard but now I rich.' I know everybody take care me when I old. My dream go home rich man. I work few years more, then I go home."

What a wonderful feeling it would have been for him to be able to boast of the wealth he had accumulated in Hawai'i to his family and friends. That would have been only natural. It would have washed away some of the pain of the sacrifices he had made for many years as a lonely man.

In many isolated areas in the country, far removed from the towns and urban areas of Hawai'i, there are graveyards of immigrants buried years ago. Their headstones have fallen and no one comes to place flowers on their graves. They had probably worked hard intending to return to their mother country, but for one reason or another, they could not return, and now, they remain in desolate, lonely places long forgotten. The trade winds crossing the land like ancient spirits floating by whisper their names as you pass.

This fire was indeed a tragedy for the unfortunate gardener. It was tragedy compounded because he was so close to reaching his goal—retirement. Now, he had nothing. It was too much for him to start all over again at such an advanced age. His dream of returning to Japan with money in his pocket was gone forever. How nice it would have been for him, if he could have returned to his family and had been able to say, "All those years of hard work in Hawai'i were years of struggle, but they were worth it. I am happy and content now. I can enjoy my remaining years with all of you, and when I die, all that I own will be yours to share." His family would have cared for him when he could no longer take care of himself.

I don't know if he ever enjoyed life. Maybe his dream of returning home as a wealthy man was so overpowering that everything else was secondary. His priority was to work hard and save enough to return to homeland. That was his goal and he was willing to give up some of the other simple pleasures of life which others take for granted, such as a family in Hawai'i, friends, a movie now and then, new clothes and such other things which makes life a bit more enjoyable.

The pain of losing his life savings was too much for him. In a month or two, we learned that the old man died, quietly in bed, staring at the ceiling, his mouth agape, his cheeks sunken in, his breathing barely audible. The minister's wife later told my mother that the old man never uttered a word, not even a sound, after the night of the fire. ◆

THE MYSTERY OF THE SECLUDED YARD

After these many years, we had finally made it into Mrs. White's yard. We stood in the middle of her large, manicured, emerald green lawn. We were awestruck by the size and grandeur of her lawn, for even in Hilo where many homes had large yards, this one was really huge, probably an acre or two. We had always suspected that it was large, but we didn't realize the extent of its depth and spaciousness. We had known that it took the gardener an entire day to mow the lawn and maintain and care for the plants on the property.

As long as we had known Mrs. White, she had lived alone. No one visited her, except a niece who came once in a great while. The only other person was a maid who cleaned her home every day. She was a short, elderly Japanese woman, who came early in the morning, long before we left for school, and left late in the evening. She reminded me of a bantam chicken, plump, constantly moving. She would walk briskly, open the gate to Mrs. White's property, step in, close the latch and disappear into the forest of plants and shrubbery in the yard. In the evening the routine would be reversed. The maid never said much. The niece was even less friendly. I do not recall the niece ever saying a word to us. She never acknowledged our presence, never waved or smiled at us.

There was a low wire fence on the street side of Mrs. White's property, but the property itself was concealed by tall trees and bushes. Even if you were to part the plants to take a peek, you could not get a good view of the yard. All this added to a mystery of the place. As all boys are, curiosity got the best of us and we would wonder what was in her yard. One thing was certain. She lived in a two-story, dark green house about a hundred yards from the street. Whenever we peered through the thick shrubbery planted on the street side of the property, we could faintly see another house on the dark, far end of the property.

"Maybe, it's a house where she's keeping someone a prisoner," suggested Thomas, one of the boys in the neighborhood.

"Nah, I bet it's a haunted house. That's what I think it is," said Andrew, the oldest boy in the group. "Maybe someone was murdered in the house, and now it's haunted." That was enough to send a cold chill through me. That wasn't exactly a cheerful thought, having something spooky right across the street from our home.

As the years went by, whenever we would be sitting in our yard with nothing to do but to let our imagination run wild, we would look across the street to Mrs. White's property and wonder among ourselves what the mysterious house was. We certainly couldn't ask Mrs. White's niece because it was really none of our business what it was. As for the maid, she couldn't be bothered with our nonsense.

One late afternoon in July, as we were playing softball in our yard, Corky, another of the neighborhood friends, hit the ball unusually hard and it flew across the street and sailed over Mrs. White's fence and into her yard. We all stood in silence, aghast. It was the only ball we had and we had to retrieve it. The question was how?

Andrew had a logical answer, "Corky, you hit it. You get it." That made a lot of sense. Since Corky hit the ball, he ought to get it.

"Yeah, but how am I going to get it?" he asked.

"That's your problem. You didn't have to hit it so hard, you know," replied Andrew.

I said a silent prayer of thanks. I was glad it wasn't my problem. I wouldn't have known how to get into Mrs. White's yard. I know I couldn't have gone to her home and asked her if I could retrieve the ball. She was a very private person, and we had rarely ever seen her. Sometimes we would see a white-haired woman walking slowly with a cane in the yard. We presumed it was Mrs. White. There were mango and cheery trees in her yard, but she had never invited us to pick the fruits. She kept to herself.

Corky crossed the street slowly with his head hung low like a condemned prisoner. We all knew that retrieving the ball meant trespassing in Mrs. White's private property. Even worse was the fact that it might mean searching for the ball in the vicinity of the mysterious house in the dark corner of the yard. It made me shudder to even think about it.

Corky made a running leap like an athlete training for the Olympics high jump and cleared the fence and fell into the shrubbery. We couldn't see him, nor did we hear anything. My heart stopped cold, as we waited for Corky. *What courage,* I thought. As we waited, the seconds seemed like hours. The minutes passed excruciatingly slowly. I thought the worse. Was he captured and made a prisoner in the mysterious house? Was he harmed? Or, the very worst, was he d-e-a-d? When you don't know what's happening your mind conjures up horrible thoughts, usually the worst.

What seemed like a million hours later, Corky appeared suddenly in the shrubbery. We all jumped back. We could only see his head. His face was smiling. My god! This was weird. What happened to the rest of his body?

He spoke, "Hey, you guys. It's really a different kind of place. Come on."

"What do you mean, a different kind of place?" I asked.

"I can't quite explain. You gotta to see for yourself. That's all I can say. Hurry up," Corky replied.

"What about the ball?" my brother asked. It was his ball and it was important for him to retrieve the ball.

"Don't worry. I got the ball. I even got to see the mystery house," Corky said.

I asked, "Did you see anyone in the house?"

"There's no one in the house. In fact, there's nothing in the house. Come on. Quickly. Come and see the house for yourself. It's an unusual house. Never saw anything like it before in my life."

"What do you mean?" asked Thomas.

"Instead of asking me questions, come and see it for yourself."

"You think we should? It's private property, you know," I said to no one in particular.

By this time, we were all curious to see the mystery house and since nothing had happened to Corky, certainly nothing could happen to us. Our curiosity was so overwhelming that we were willing to risk the danger of going onto forbidden territory to satisfy our curiosity. Even at the expense of breaking the law. We all took a running leap over the fence and landed in the soft shrubbery. Corky led the way to an opening. Lo and behold! This was another world. It was a fantastically, huge yard with Mrs. White's home standing under an old, sprawling lychee tree. The yard was well maintained. The grass was cut evenly and the shrubbery was all neatly trimmed. Not like ours, with the parts of the lawn brown from us running from home plate to first base, second base, third base and then toward home plate again. We crossed the lawn in the fading, summer sunlight toward the mystery house. After all these years of guessing, our mystery was to be solved.

We crept carefully down a slight slope and there in the corner of the yard stood the mystery house. Corky was right. There was no one in it and there was nothing in it. We all stood and stared at it. We had never seen a house like it, and it wouldn't be until years later when I would see another one like it. I had not even seen pictures of a house like this. No, you couldn't really refer to it as a house. It was more like a small bandstand in the park. It was shaped like an octagon with the front open, and the remaining sides had latticed walls.

"I don't think anyone lives in this house," my brother suggested.

"That's for sure," said Andrew.

"I wonder what Mrs. White does here," I asked.

Obviously, we couldn't very well ask her.

It was to be many, many years later that I was to learn that the mystery house was nothing more than a gazebo, but in those days, not many people had a gazebo and I don't think there are many people today who have a gazebo in their yard for that matter. But, at least, we learned what the mystery house was.

With nothing having happened to us in Mrs. White's secluded yard, we had tasted the forbidden fruit and we had not been burnt for our transgressions. Hey! This wasn't too bad.

Corky yelled out, "Let's toss the ball around."

He threw the ball far and wide to my brother, who tossed it high to Andrew, who pitched it to me and I flung it to Thomas. We threw the ball high in the air, and whoever caught it would throw it as high as he could. We started getting loud and boisterous.

Thomas discovered a tree loaded down with dark purple berries, which we all tasted. They were juicy. There was so much juice in the berries; the juice flowed down our hands leaving a purple stain. We must have each eaten more than a handful when we started throwing the berries at each other. When the berries hit a target, they splattered and made a purple splotch, a real mess. Pretty soon, the yard was strewn with smashed berries. The messier it got, the more excited we hooligans became by this act of vandalism. We all looked like purple spotted creatures. We yelled and hollered, having so much fun.

Then, a voice rang out, "Get out of my yard! You criminals! This is private property. You are trespassing. I will call the police to arrest you if you don't leave now." There stood a white-haired woman supported by a cane on the porch. It was Mrs. White.

POLICE! My god! The POLICE! She called us criminals. Arrest! Holy smoke. Wait! She was absolutely right. We were criminals. We broke the law. We trespassed on her private property. The law! The impact of that word was like a bolt of lightning from the Old Testament heaven striking me down. In those days, the word "law" meant something. The law was to be obeyed. Breaking the law meant severe, dire consequences. I could see Daddy and Mama standing beside me at court. Mama crying. Daddy grim. Oh, why, oh, why, did we ever commit a crime? It is amazing how many terror-filled thoughts can crowd into a space of a second. Court, the judge, prison. We would have hell to pay. Oh, god! I trembled at the thought of spending time behind bars.

"You bad boys!" cried out Mrs. White.

Oh, god! Bad. Yes, yes. We are bad. We really didn't mean to do it. Honest, Mrs. White, if you get to know us, we're really not bad, really. Oh, forgive us. Please let us go this time. I promise never to go into your yard again. Never, never, never. My mind screamed with remorse.

My heart pumped hard and my legs suddenly became rubbery. My knees buckled under me. I had to get out at all cost. My legs were like newly poured cement—fluid, but hardening quickly by the second. They weren't moving fast enough for me. Oh, legs and feet, carry me home and I promise to be a good and law-abiding citizen forever and ever. I promise. I could not afford to get arrested. We all scampered out the yard as fast as our youthful legs could carry us, each boy for himself.

I had terrible visions as I ran like a rabbit fleeing to escape a rapacious wolf. What would my father say if we got arrested? He had admonished us, "We may not be rich, but we have a good reputation. The Kodani name has not been tarnished and you must never do anything that will bring a black mark against our name. In life, a good name is very, very important. Sometimes, it is more important than all the money in the world. Once you do anything bad, people will not forget. It is very hard to erase a bad mark against you. You must never do anything that might bring shame to the family. It's not only you who is ruined, but the shame will cause disgrace to the whole family. It affects us all. Don't be tempted to do anything that might be fun in the beginning but will bring nothing but trouble later. The grief is not worth the brief moment of pleasure."

What if I am arrested? I thought. My father would never forgive me for bringing dishonor and grievous shame to the family. He had worked so hard to give us a good home and the comforts of life, and now by our foolishness, we were to be arrested.

We ran at full speed. We jumped over the fence. No, we flew over the fence. We all ran like we had never run before. This was a nightmare! Driven by fear, and yet our legs and feet, not quite being able to handle the demands of our fear. *Feet, move faster, faster,* I pleaded. Still, it was not fast enough for me. The other boys dashed ahead of me. I could feel my heart pounding, and I could actually hear it pounding. It was like a slow motion movie. I strained to move faster, but I didn't seem to be making any progress. I hardly seemed to be moving. My mouth was dry. My hands were drenched with sweat. I dared not look back. Could the police have already arrived? Pure terror. Believe you me, this was fear in its purest form. We, criminals, scattered. Each raced home, home to our sanctuary. You never appreciate home until you realize that you may not get to go home.

My father was in the garden as I ran home—to safe harbor. The first shades of night crossed the evening sky.

"What happened, Roy? You're flushed. Are you feeling all right?" my father asked.

"Yes. Of course, why do you ask?"

"You don't look like your usual self, that's why. And, what's all that mess on you?"

"Nothing, Dad," I answered.

"Well, I think you're going to hear it from Mama. Are you sure you're feeling all right? You don't look too good."

"I'm OK. I was just running. Everything is OK."

"Where's Jimmy?"

"He ran into the house, Dad," I answered.

"You boys have been doing a lot of running, huh?"

"That's for sure, Dad."

I looked toward Mrs. White's home. Everything looked normal. No police. No juvenile delinquent investigators. Nothing. It was the close of another summer day, quiet and peaceful. Nothing extraordinary happened that day in the history of the world. It was just another ordinary day. But, for me, it was a day to mark in my calendar as a day of lessons learned. ◆

MY FATHER, THE LOBBYIST

I n this season of politics and election campaigns waged by politicians, I am reminded of the time my father was a lobbyist for Big Island (Hawai'i Island) farmers in the Territorial Legislature in the mid-1940s. From the late 1930s and for about ten years thereafter, my father, Asao, was the manager of Hilo Farmers Exchange, often referred to as "FX," on Keawe Street in Hilo right across from K. Taniguchi Store. FX was a cooperative association of farmers that sold their farm produce to FX, which in turn acted as a wholesaler and shipped most of the produce to Honolulu. Most of the farmers were issei from Hiroshima and their farms were located in Waimea. The names of farmers I recall now are Hori, Hirako, Hirayama, Kawano, Okura, Okada, Oye, Fukuki, Onodera, Masake, Hara, Eguchi and Ishihara.

At that time, a flower called *akulekule* in colors of white, blue, pink, lavender and orange grew in great abundance like a Persian carpet all over the yards in Waimea. As the song goes, I wonder where the flowers have gone? Waimea still has a special place in my heart. The weather is cool most of the time and the hills are emerald green. It reminds me of the countryside of Connecticut or western Massachusetts.

Until 1946, when the tsunami wiped out roads and the railroads along the Hāmākua Coast, Māmalahoa Highway was a two-lane road with few bridges. The farmers would depart Waimea in the early morning hours in the dark and arrive in Hilo about 6:30 or 7 a.m. During the war, it was dangerous to drive the trucks with the headlights partially covered on roads that twisted and turned at every Hāmākua gulch.

Until I was about four years old, I only spoke Japanese because I played among the farmers who only spoke Japanese, mostly in the Hiroshima dialect.

I do not know what legislation the farmers had wished to enact, but a group of them and my father went to Honolulu to seek legislation that would assist the farmers. At that time, the Territorial Legislature convened in 'Iolani Palace, the only palace in the United States, and they went to meet the senator who chaired the Agriculture Committee. His name will remain confidential for obvious reasons to be explained later. This was before sunshine laws and ethics regulating the conduct of legislators.

The farmers and my father were warmly greeted by the senator. As my father later told the story, the senator seemed to be a busy man who did not waste time extending cordialities. He did not mince words and came straight to the point, "What you guys want?"

The senior farmer explained the problem and requested the senator's *kōkua* (assistance) in introducing legislation to assist the farmers. Politics then was raw politics. Politicians did not mess around with pulled punches. A spade was a spade.

The senator then asked, "What you guys wen bring me?"

My father pulled out a bottle of whiskey. During the war, whiskey could only be acquired with ration cards that were presented to the stores designated with a special license. My father always sent my mother to buy whisky as *omiyage* (gift or souvenir), which was a highly prized gift. As my mother would tell us years later, "I was so shame to stand in line to buy whiskey. People who saw me in line would yell out, 'Oh, Mrs. Kodani, enjoy your whiskey.' So shame. Those days, women did not drink whiskey or beer. I don't even drink coffee."

My father, with a grand gesture, placed the bottle on the senator's desk thinking the senator would be happy to receive such gift.

The senator looked at it. He didn't say a word. He just grimaced as though afflicted with a stomach ailment. "You guys want me to help you, huh?"

Everyone nodded in agreement.

"You guys wen bring me one bottle of whiskey?"

Again, everyone nodded in agreement.

"You know what? In Hilo, you guys have dried *akule* (a kind of fish), yeah?"

The senior farmer replied, "Oh, yes, Senatuh, we get plenty dried akule."

"OK, den, you guys go wrap the dried akule in the newspaper and go bring the dried akule to me. Den, we talk again. You guys know what I mean, huh?"

As my father tells the story, nobody could understand why the senator wanted dried akule from Hilo because there were dried akule in Honolulu too.

Because the farmers and my father didn't seem to understand what he meant, the senator said, "You guys really slow, yeah? Bring me three big dried akule. OK?"

Then, the light came on. Now everyone understood what the three big dried akule meant. They all interpreted it to mean $300, but as my father would later say, you could pay $2,000 and buy a parcel of land and build a nice house in Hilo for that sum of money. $300 was quite substantial at that time.

The farmers and my father stepped outside to consider the senator's proposal. They all agreed $300 was too much, far too much, to pay for new legislation. They never went back to ask the senator's kōkua.

This is a true story of my father's experience as a lobbyist in the Territorial Legislature. Every time he ate dried akule as *pūpū* (appetizer) with his beer with the farmers in Hilo, he would say, "*Nani ka* (somehow) this dried akule no taste the same like before."

And the farmers all nodded in agreement. One of the farmers inevitably would comment, "Dat senatuh was one *hoito* (Hiroshima dialect meaning greedy) buggah. Just imagine. He was elected to serve da public. Maybe I should quit farming and become a politician instead. Anytime anybody need my kōkua, they bring me dried akule."

All the other farmers laughed uproariously. ◆

WHEN DOGS DO NOT HOWL

This story begins long before I was born, long before my parents had even met. It really starts when my mother was in her teens.

Sumi was one of my mother's closest friends. Both were of the same age and they lived in the same sugar plantation camp about three miles from the town of Pāpaʻikou, located on the road that circles the island. When my mother was growing up in the late 1920s, all the children in the camp walked to school and back home each day. There was no such thing as a school bus. Even the adults walked to town. Only a few wealthy individuals owned a car, but then, there weren't wealthy Asian immigrants in Hawaiʻi. It is hard to believe, but a car, which we take for granted now was a luxury then. The road to my mother's camp, if you could call it a road, was actually a wide trail. It was neither concrete nor macadamized. Walking on the road was difficult because of the rocks and potholes. When it rained, the road turned into a raging river and made walking even more difficult.

Sumi was the eldest of four girls in her family. Sumi's father was a determined man. His heart was set on having a male heir and he kept on trying until a son was born. His determination caused consternation to Sumi's mother. She was worried that each of the children would be a daughter. Then, what was she to do? Well, finally, a son was born and Sumi's father was overjoyed. He was named Hajime, the beginning.

As Hajime grew, Sumi's father was the proudest man in the camp. Hajime was the splitting image of his father. Not only did he look like his father, but he also walked like his father and as he grew older, he talked like his father, slowly and precisely. Hajime could do no wrong in his father's eyes.

Hajime had a normal childhood. He did all the things that boys his age did during those days in Hawaiʻi. There was nothing extraordinary or abnormal about him. He was just an average boy. If you were to look at him, he had a mischievous twinkle in his eyes, and he appeared fit and healthy. You could not help but to like Hajime. He was such a cheerful and personable youngster.

Then, one morning, as my mother recalls, as the children were getting ready to leave the camp for school, Hajime could not be found. His sister searched everywhere for him. There was absolutely no trace of him. He had simply disappeared. He was about seven or eight years old then. He just disappeared from the face of the earth, as though a mysterious force plucked him out of bed and carried him off to some far away land. At first, everyone called out to him, but there was no answer. Then, groups were organized and the adults spent the day looking for Hajime everywhere. As to be expected, when something mysterious like this occurs, the people in the camp became frightened, apprehensive and worried. As the sun set that day, the night wind from the mountains whipped over the camp. Parents called out for their children. There was no telling what might happen. Hajime's father turned sullen overnight, spoke to no one, and from that day on he walked with his head hanging low, never looked up, even when you talked to him. He stared at the ground. He seemed oblivious to everything around him. Some said the loss of his son was too much for Sumi's father to bear.

The people in the camp said that Hajime was just a young boy. They agreed he couldn't have just disappeared into thin air, and so, they continued to search for him, looking farther and farther from camp. Some said, "He must have walked in his sleep. He must be in the cane fields somewhere." Others said, "He must have run away from home for some reason, whatever the reason may be." They searched for days. Friends and relatives from town came to help in the search. He was nowhere to be found.

As my mother remembers, Sumi would call out as the sun set each day, "Hajime! Hajime! Hajime!" As she called, everyone in the camp would stop whatever they were doing and listen breathlessly, waiting for a response. She would call out until she was too exhausted to cry out for him. Sumi's mother and father never called out for him. The neighbors said that they were too grief stricken to call out his name.

The search continued for several weeks. They looked every possible place where they thought he might be. They retraced their steps to be sure they had not overlooked any crevice he may have fallen into. Still, he was not found.

In the light of a kerosene lantern late one evening, the camp boss out of the presence of Sumi's parents said, "I have a feeling he is alive."

"How do you know? Is there something you haven't told us?" the others asked the boss.

"What usually happens when someone dies?" asked the boss.

"What are you talking about?" the others asked.

"I have been listening every night and I wait and wait patiently. I hear nothing. Only the sound of the wind."

"Do you expect Hajime to answer Sumi when she calls out for him?"

"No, I don't. I wait to hear something which I haven't heard yet."

"Get to the point. What are you waiting to hear?"

"I wait for the dogs."

"What about the dogs?"

"I wait to hear the howling of the dogs, but have any of you noticed? The dogs have not howled since Hajime disappeared. We all know dogs howl, usually at night, when someone dies. Has anyone heard the dogs howl?"

"Now that you mention it. You are right. If he is not dead, where can he be?" someone asked. "I sure hope he is not somewhere suffering in pain."

The boss replied, "I really don't know where he could be. I can't figure this out."

The days turned into weeks, and the weeks into months and the months into years. Life goes on, and everyone has his own problems to worry about. Other things became more pressing. Gradually, people forgot about Hajime and went on with their lives. After Hajime's disappearance, Sumi's family no longer socialized with the rest of the camp. They kept to themselves. Sumi's parents suddenly turned old and gray. Young as they were, even Sumi and her sisters took on very mature facial features.

Sumi nor any of her sisters ever married.

When I was growing up, Sumi would walk by my father's hardware store and stop now and then and chat with my mother. She was a thin woman, with a slight stoop and gray hair gathered in the back in a bun. I never saw her smile. I once remarked to my mother, "Ma, your friend, Sumi, looks like a zombie. What's the matter with her?"

"She lost a brother long ago when he was about your age. She has never forgotten him, Roy. Some people never forget about their brother or sister."

"It seems that she stopped living after her brother died," I said. "She walks around without any life in her. She doesn't have any pep."

"Her family took it real hard. I guess even after all these years they have not quite been able to lead a normal life. Sumi was the prettiest girl in the camp. She could have married any man, but she never got married. I know she would have been a good wife and mother. I'm sure several men proposed to her, but she never accepted any of them. I never could understand why. Sometimes, life has a strange way of turning and twisting in a way we never ever expected."

About twenty years after that conversation, after I had become an attorney practicing in Honolulu, my mother telephoned me and asked if I could help Sumi.

"How can I help her? What's the problem?" I asked.

"Her father died a few days ago and she and her sisters want you to help them with the assets he owned when he died. Sumi and her sisters are worried because he had no will. They're afraid having no will might cause an inheritance problem."

"It's not a problem. His assets will be divided and distributed to the beneficiaries according to law," I replied.

The following day I took a late plane to Hilo, and after the funeral, I met with Sumi and her sisters. To alleviate any concerns that they might have, I explained that having no will was not an insurmountable problem. Under the laws of intestacy, the law designates the beneficiaries of a person who has died, unlike a will or trust in which the owner of assets can choose his beneficiaries. "Under the Hawai'i law, all brothers and sisters share and share alike," I said. "There are four of you, and so, each of you will get a one-fourth share."

I took out my yellow legal pad and began taking the necessary information. "I need to get all of your names and addresses. I understand your mother died many years ago. And, just to be sure, is there anyone else I should list as a beneficiary?"

The sisters looked at each other. *What is going on?* I wondered. Sumi cleared her throat as though choking on something. She spoke hesitatingly, "Yes, could you also list as one of the beneficiaries—Joe Chin."

"Joe Chin," I repeated. "What's his address?"

Sumi looked down at the ground as though searching for something and said almost inaudibly, "Kalaupapa, Moloka'i."

"Kalaupapa, Moloka'i?" I repeated to be sure.

"Yes," Sumi answered.

"Is Joe Chin a patient there?" I asked.

All the sisters looked at each other, and hesitantly they answered, "Yes."

It all dawned on me instantly at that moment. Kalaupapa, Moloka'i was the Hansen's disease, or leprosy, settlement in Hawai'i.

"Joe Chin is your brother, isn't he?"

All the sisters nodded their heads to indicate that he was in fact their brother, Hajime.

"Has he lived there all of his life?" I asked.

"Yes, he has. We all feel so shame he has that disease. My father had him change his name so that nobody would ever know he was related to us."

"There are drugs that can help him now."

"But when Hajime got it there was no help, and this is why they didn't want any of us to get married because they were worried that one of us might also get the same disease, and we might pass it on to our children."

"He was very young, I suppose, when he went to Kalaupapa?"

"Oh, yes, he was," replied one of the sisters.

"How did you find out that he had Hansen's disease?"

Sumi looked at her sisters, as though wanting their approval to speak on the matter. Having kept her brother's condition a secret all these years was too much for her. She spoke with great relief of a tremendous burden cast aside, "As you may remember when you used to visit your grandmother's home at the camp, we used to wash clothes outside. We would boil water in a large tub over a fire and soak the dirty clothes in the boiling water. We would then take the clothes out and scrub them on a washboard until the clothes were clean. Then, we would rinse the clothes in cold, clean water. Well, one day while Hajime was playing nearby while my mother and I were washing clothes, he wanted to put more wood in the fire. You know how children love to play with fire. My mother said all right. He got some firewood and put them in the fire, but as he did so he accidentally stepped on a burning firewood. But, to our horror, he didn't cry out or anything. He had not felt the burning firewood. I was too young to know, but my mother knew instantly. It was because his skin was insensitive to heat. She knew right away that he had leprosy."

"How was Hajime taken to Kalaupapa?"

"My mother told us the story years later, when I first fell in love with this wonderful boy. My mother had to tell me why I shouldn't be thinking about boys or about marriage. My father never talked about it, never once. According to my mother, my father told Hajime that he was going to take Hajime to Hilo, and of course, those days going to Hilo was like going to the big city. Hajime was very excited. My father told him he had to get up early in the morning to catch the train to Hilo. Hajime believed him. Why shouldn't he? And so they got up early in the morning and my father took him to Pāpaʻikou where the plantation doctor was waiting for Hajime. He then arranged to take Hajime to Hilo and then to Kalaupapa. My father hurried home before anyone in the camp got up. No one ever found out about this."

"How did Hajime react to all this?"

"He was only seven or eight years old, you must remember. He was very confused and when my father left him with the doctor he began crying. My father said he would come and get him when he got well."

Hajime said, "But, Papa, I don't feel sick or anything. Why must I stay with the doctor when I am not sick?"

My father couldn't say anything. And so, the doctor tried to help by answering, "There are some illness that you don't necessarily feel sick but in truth you are. You have such an illness, Hajime."

"What happened after that?" I inquired.

"Well, Hajime would write letters to us. Short letters in his boyish scrawl. Always asking to come home."

"Did anyone answer his letters?"

"No. My father said to burn the letters. He warned us never to talk about Hajime to anyone. He said as far as he was concerned Hajime had died. But the letters continued to come. He pleaded with my father to come and get him. He said he wanted to come home. My father ordered us not to write to him. I guess because no one wrote back, his letters became fewer and fewer. As time went on, he must have realized he could never return home. In one of his last letters, Hajime asked if we still thought about him. My father yelled at me for reading his letter and ordered me, "Burn the damn letter." He stalked out of the house and slammed the door. I can still see my mother standing by the kitchen door squeezing the white apron she had on with tears in her eyes and her mouth quivering trying not to cry. A few minutes later as I went out to burn the letter, I heard someone crying by the wood shed. I crept to see who it was. I couldn't believe it. It was my father. He was sitting on the ground with his head in both hands and he was crying uncontrollably. I knew then that even with all the shouting and ranting to forget Hajime my father cared deeply for Hajime, that he loved Hajime, as only a father could love his children, but he was frustrated because there was nothing he could do to help Hajime. As I thought about it years later, it might have been worse for Hajime to give him false hope that he could eventually return home when he got well, because in my father's heart, he knew that Hajime could never get better, only worse. I'm sure Hajime suffered all these years, but I know that my mother and father also suffered great pain because they felt so helpless."

Oh, yes, one final matter. Years later after the father's estate was probated, the Department of Health changed its policy and allowed all Hansen's disease patients to leave Kalaupapa and move to a hospital near Honolulu, if the patient desired to do so. However, because Hajime had spent a greater part of his life in Kalaupapa, he decided to remain and spend the rest of his life there. By then, he considered Kalaupapa to be his home.

Sumi told me, "One time I took a small airplane to Kalaupapa to see Hajime. He had his own house and he was living alone. He was about forty-five years old, not the young boy I remembered. After all these years, I wanted to hold him, to hug him. In my heart he was still my little brother. When I tried to reach over to him, he took a step back. I spent the day with him, but we didn't have much to say to each other. I asked him, 'Do you need anything, Hajime?' He said, 'I have everything I need.' 'Do you want me to say anything to your sisters?' 'I was so young when I left the camp. I don't remember my sisters. I don't even know you.' 'Is there anything I can do for you,' I asked. 'Yes, please don't ever come again. I am not blaming you, or Otosan or Okasan for anything. It's just that I cried so much when I first came here. I was so lonely. I thought I was abandoned. I know nobody could help me. This is now my life. If you come again, I will remember how sad and lonely I was as a young boy. The Catholic sisters tried to make me comfortable, but I was so lonely. You don't know how it feels to be lonely, especially when you are young. I don't want to remember those days.'" ♦

SHE DIED BEFORE SHE ACTUALLY DIED

"Do you know how my mother died?" Betty (not her real name) asked me. She was a few years older than I, and we had both attended Hilo Hongwanji Japanese Language School. Betty was a studious and serious student at the school. Most of the boys, including me, attended Japanese language school, because we had to, because our parents required us to. The irony of it all is now I spend a lot of my professional life communicating in Japanese. If I had studied more diligently I would be able to read and write more *kanji* (Chinese characters) than I do at the present time.

My wife, my two daughters and I were at the Hilo Farmers' Market on the corner of Kamehameha Avenue and Mamo Street looking to buy papayas and other fruits to bring back with us to Honolulu, when Betty called out to me in the crowd, "Roy, is that you?"

A few months after her mother died, Betty, her sister and father moved, and I had lost track of her, but even after all those years, I knew it was Betty. Her eyes still sparkled, and she had a warm smile. Some people never change.

When my daughters were young, my wife, daughters and I would go to Hilo a week or so before New Year's Day to help my parents and my uncle, Takashi, pound mochi. It was an annual event until my mother said, "I think we have to stop pounding mochi."

"Why?" I asked.

"It's getting too much for me to carry the mochi rice from the kitchen upstairs to the downstairs garage."

When I think about it now, I wonder why it was my mother who had to carry the cooked mochi rice wrapped in cotton gauze? We pounded about eleven to twelve times. Why couldn't I have carried them? Those who have pounded mochi know it is strenuous work heaving the *kine* (wooden pounder) or grinding kine against the *usu* (mortar).

My father stored the usu and kine in the garage until mochi-pounding time each year. I know Uncle Takashi carved the head of the kine from the milo wood, but I wonder who had carved the usu out of the hard rock? That too would be an interesting story.

My daughters loved to help my mother shape the sticky mochi into round mochi. My mother would always say, "If you want your children to be beautiful or handsome, be sure to make your mochi nice and round." Love of mochi is in our blood, because now my *hapa* (mixed race) granddaughter and grandson enjoy eating mochi.

After pounding mochi, my family and I would always go to the farmers' market, because in part it was a family tradition, although my daughters weren't enthused about it.

Betty and I chatted with people milling around us. The farmers' market has not changed in all these years. After a rain, the ground is soaked and wet. Parts of it are still pebbles and soil. My daughters were getting fidgety.

When Betty suddenly blurted out her question about her mother, I thought, *Why did she have to ask about her mother's death in the presence of my two young daughters?* Her mother had died over twenty-five years ago, for that matter. I wasn't even a close friend of hers. We had just gone to Japanese language school together.

"Today is my mother's *meinichi* (death memorial day). I try to come to Hilo and go *hakamairi* (attend the grave) at least once a year. I came to buy some flowers for her grave."

I looked over her shoulder toward Hilo Bay, and I recalled a hushed conversation between my mother and father in the parlor when I must have been in the second or third grade at Hilo Union School. It was just before I fell asleep, between consciousness and dropping off to sleep, when I think I remember my mother saying, "Daddy, you know Mrs. Kato (a fictitious name) died yesterday?"

"Yeah, too bad. She was not old. They have two young daughters around Roy's age. *Kawaiso* (sad) for the husband and daughters. Was she sick or somet'ing?"

"That's the thing."

"Whatch you mean?"

"I saw her neighbor today at the fish market."

"So?"

"Hard to understand."

"Whatcha talking about?"

"The neighbor said the younger daughter came running to their house after school. She was crying and screaming. When the daughter came home, she couldn't find the mother. Usually the mother is home, and the older sister goes to Japanese school. So, the younger daughter looked all over house for Mrs. Kato."

"And?"

"She went downstairs to the *furo* (bath) room. And...the poor daughter..."

"Da poor daughter what?"

"She found the mother near the furo."

"Well, I'm happy she found da mother."

"No. That's the terrible part. I don't know why she would do something terrible like that."

"Like what?"

"Mrs. Kato hanged herself."

"What?"

"Yes, Daddy, the poor daughter had to find her mother...hanging."

My father sighed, "Mr. and Mrs. Kato always seem to be a happy couple. Dey were always together. She was a nice, quiet lady. She didn't talk too much. It couldn't be just a fight between husband and wife. To commit suicide, you must be beyond thinking straight. What mother would commit suicide knowing she would leave behind two young daughters?"

As I dozed off to sleep, my mother's last question was, "I wonder why she did that?"

Even today I don't know why Betty asked me about her mother's death. Maybe she wanted to unload her deep, dark, oppressive burden to someone after these many years? Maybe she thought an attorney would understand her burden more than anyone else. I don't know why she asked me.

I realized that this was not a mere chitchat between two friends, and so I told my wife to take our daughters to Café Pesto a few doors down, famous for its pizza and pasta.

"Roy, you seem to know how my mother died."

"I was young when your mother died, I'm not sure."

"She committed suicide by hanging herself."

I have learned that often times it is best not to say anything when a person wishes to talk, because the person will speak at his or her own pace and bring out at his or her own tempo what lies in the deepest recesses of that person's mind and memory.

"For years I could not forgive my mother for hanging herself in the house. Why do it in the house? She must have known that either my sister or I would find her before my father came home from work. From that day, my sister would not go downstairs. At night she would scream in her sleep. I couldn't go downstairs to take a bath. Even my father stopped taking a bath downstairs. We would go to my grandmother's house at night to take a bath. I asked my father why my mother hanged herself, and he would just shake his head. He couldn't talk about it."

"Betty, after all these years, do you think you know why your mother committed suicide? As I recall, your mother and father seemed to get along well."

"It bothered me for a long time. That's the only thing I could think about. I used to think that maybe it was something I did, and I would feel so bad. But, we were good kids. We studied hard and we obeyed my mother and father. I couldn't think why she would do such a thing that would cause so much pain for my father, my sister and me."

"Maybe she was depressed?"

"Maybe she was, but she would be shame to talk to a psychiatrist in those days. I don't even know if there was a psychiatrist in Hilo then."

"Is that why you moved?"

"Yes, we just couldn't live in that house. My father tried to sell the house, but nobody would buy the house, even for a cheap price. Eventually, a retired haole couple from the Mainland bought the house, almost free."

I asked, "I wonder what was the reason for causing your mother to do such a thing?"

Betty answered, "Everybody used to say that my parents were such a loving couple. They always seem to be happy together. But, that was outside the house. At home my father and mother didn't talk too much to each other. They didn't fight. They didn't argue or anything like that. I don't think there was any money problem. They slept in the same bedroom. My father was an electrician, he worked for the county and he would take outside jobs for extra money. He was a hard-working man. He didn't drink or cause any problem for my mother that I know. I don't think he denied her anything. Another thing about my father."

"Yes, what about him?"

"He never remarried. You know why?"

"I don't know."

"There were several women who felt sorry for my sister and me, and I think they would have married my father because he was a kind person, but... There was a stigma or something. No woman in Hilo at that time would many a man whose first wife had committed suicide. My mother's suicide may not have been his fault, but there was a dark cloud over my father."

It was obvious to me that Betty probably knew why her mother had committed suicide, and so, I asked her again, "Betty, why do you think your mother did such a thing?"

"I thought about it and thought about it. I read books and I studied psychology in college. The only conclusion I reach is that...after a while my mother really had no reason to live. Nothing, not even her two daughters. Inside she had just dried up. In Hilo it rains a lot, but inside of her, it was a desert. Every day was the same for her, monotonous. Maybe she felt she was in a prison, nowhere to go, nothing to do. Same, same, all the time. She used to talk to the neighbor lady, but I don't think she had really close friends. She was a very private person. You know, Roy, you got to have some pleasure in your life. To be human, you got to have pain, some feelings, good or bad. You may not like it, but you got to be upset at something sometimes. At least, you have some emotion. If you have nothing, then you have nothing to get up in the morning for. I ask my children, 'What do you like to do?' My son loves sports. My daughter likes her science projects. At least, they have something they like to do. In my mother's case, every day was the same routine. Some women may be satisfied with that kind of life, but I really think emotionally she had died long before she actually died. Inside she was empty." ♦

FAR AWAY BUT NOT FORGOTTEN

I have never met the person whom I write about, nor do I remember his name. He is someone whom his brother told me about, many years ago when I was attending Hilo High School. Whenever I see the declining number of veterans of the 100th Battalion and the 442nd Infantry Regiment, I wonder what has happened to him, whether he is still living or has died. For purposes of this story, I will refer to him as Sergeant.

During the summers of my high school years, I worked as a field hand at Kea'au Macadamia Nut Orchard, owned then by Castle & Cooke. I worked with other high school boys and earned the same wage as a regular new hire, about $49 a week. We worked in the hot summer sun, spreading fertilizer by hand, controlling weeds by brushing herbicide over acres and acres of land with macadamia nut trees. This experience motivated me to go to college. I was not cut out to work in the fields in the hot sun.

My father who owned a hardware store on Kilauea Avenue in Hilo, insisted I have the experience of working for someone else. He said, "You must go out and learn to eat from another man's *chawan* (rice bowl)."

I believe young boys learn sound values from their parents, relatives and church, but a young boy learns about the realities of life by listening to older men talk about life and people, subjects not ordinarily discussed at the family dining table.

I learned about life and people during the lunch breaks at the Kea'au Macadamia Nut Orchard listening to the older workers. I learned that in sugar plantation camps, the residents knew what was going on, even if they did not actually see what was happening in the house. Somehow they knew.

Knowledge and information were limited then. Television had just started broadcasting in black and white in Hilo. It was difficult for a teenager to acquire information about the human body and sex from a reliable source. Mostly, such information was through hear-say or from boys who bragged about their experiences, which in many cases were figments of their imagination.

My first summer, I used to get a ride with one of my Hilo High classmates. The radio in the car broadcasted the most popular songs at that time, such as "Hound Dog" by Elvis Presley. Another was "Rock Around The Clock" by Bill Haley and the Comets. This was the beginning of a new era of music that shocked the airwaves with rock and roll, which was a new kind of music.

One of the summer high school field hands was a student attending a military school in California or Arizona. He had all the attributes of a young officer...tall, lean, ramrod straight and silent like Clint Eastwood. His name was Mark. He only spoke when spoken to, in contrast to another summer field hand who constantly chattered like a mynah bird, even when walking alone between the rows of macadamia nut trees.

During one break, Mr. Ogamori, the field superintendent who fought in Europe during the war, asked Mark, "So, you planning to go into the infantry?"

Mark answered, "No, sir, I am going into the tank corps."

Mr. Ogamori raised his hands high toward the sky, "Are you serious? Have you been in one of those cramped, tight, airless tanks?"

"No, sir, not yet. I will do that when I go for my military training as an officer."

Mr. Ogamori looking straight at Mark said, "Well, let me tell you. When I was in Italy, I saw guys in the tanks who got blasted by rockets. The lucky ones got out, hurt maybe, but they got out. Others couldn't get out. They were cooked like pigs in an *imu* (ground pit). Even now, after all those years, I don't want to think about those tank guys."

That same summer there was an older field hand in our summer group. If I remember correctly, he was between jobs, and he wanted to be hired as a permanent worker, and so he was starting with us, the young rookies. He must have been in his late thirties at that time. I cannot remember his name, but I will refer to him as Mr. Arakawa in this story. One afternoon when it seemed that the sun was closer to Earth than usual, he and I happened to go to the truck at the same time to get a drink of water from the five-gallon aluminum water container. We all drank from the top of the container used like a cup.

Mr. Arakawa passed the cup to me and asked, "So, Kodani, what you going to do after you graduate from high school?"

"I'm planning to go to college and to law school, if my father will pay for me."

Mr. Arakawa then said, "A lot of boys who cannot afford to go to college join the Army, and use the GI Bill to go to college after their military commitment. But, if your father can help you, don't join the Army. There's no war now, but you can never tell, there might be a war when you are in the Army. Then what?"

I remember this conversation even today. I stood in the shadow of the truck, not knowing what to say. Several minutes passed, and he didn't say anything, and I had nothing to say.

Then, Mr. Arakawa took off his *lauhala* (pandanus leaf) hat that shielded him from the hot sun and spoke very quietly, "I have a brother, who was a sergeant in the Army. He got busted up real bad in France. I think they went into the forest to save some guys from Texas. I think the local guys were cannon fodders. The Army couldn't send the Mainland boys because the politicians would have raised hell. My brother almost died. I really don't know how he survived his battle wounds."

I didn't say anything. What can a fifteen-year-old teenager say to someone whose brother barely survived his war wounds?

Mr. Arakawa continued, "The other day when the guys were talking about tanks and war and death, I had a hard time just standing by them and listening. I don't like to hear about war experiences because of my brother."

I asked, "Is your brother OK now?"

Mr. Arakawa took out his handkerchief to wipe the sweat off his brow and then when I looked again, he seemed to be wiping tears flowing down his cheeks.

"From France, he was sent to an Army hospital in Michigan. My mother was so happy he was alive that she wanted to go to see him, but we didn't have enough money and the airplane ticket was expensive and in those days it was far to travel to Michigan. My father died during the war, and so he never knew what happened to my brother. Maybe it was better he never found out.

"As the months and years passed, my mother said, 'Somebody should go to see your brother. I don't want him to think we forgot him.' And so I worked two jobs, sometimes three jobs to save money to buy the airplane ticket. I had a girlfriend. She was very nice and understanding. She said she would wait for me. Later, we got married. She is a wonderful woman. Other women would not have waited years for me to save up my money for the trip to Michigan."

"Did you see your brother?" I asked.

"Yeah, it took a while, but finally I had enough money saved up and I went to see him at the hospital." He looked at the ground for several minutes as though he had lost his voice. Maybe he was too choked up to talk. I don't know.

"And what happened? He must have been happy to see you."

"I knew from the letters someone had written for him that he had been badly wounded, but I didn't realize how badly he had been wounded because he had never told us the extent of his wounds. I couldn't believe it when I saw him. He had lost both legs, his right arm was gone, and his right side was still heavily bandaged. He must have lost the right side of his upper body. He was barely able to sit up in the wheelchair. He could tell from my facial expressions that I was shocked. He asked me, 'What for you came?'

"The best I could say was, 'Okasan wanted somebody to come to let you know we still think about you all the time. She wants you to come home. She wants to take care of you at home in Hilo.' My brother replied, 'I never going home in this condition. Never, never, never. I don't want people to see me all crippled. I cannot stand to see people looking at me. Sometimes with pity. Most times, shocked.' I told him, 'If you go home, you don't have to go outside the house.' He said, 'Nobody can take care of me like the Army nurses. I don't have feelings around my stomach anymore. When I smoke and the ashes fall on my stomach, I cannot feel the ashes burning. I don't want you to come again. It is hard for you to see me, but it's more hard for me to see you staring at me with pain in your eyes. That hurts me more than the pain I have in my stomach. Thanks for coming so far to see me, but don't ever come again. Tell Okasan I am OK and I will go home soon. Don't tell her and the others about my wounds, OK?'

"The second day I visited my brother, I wheeled him to the music room, because he enjoyed music and playing the 'ukulele when he lived in Hilo. When we entered the room there was a wounded combat soldier also in a wheelchair with his head drooped on the left side of his chest. A nurse was playing a single record 'Diana' by Paul Anka. For some unexplained reason, the soldier requested the nurse to play the same record over and over. My brother didn't say anything, and we stayed in the room for about twenty minutes and then we left. But, even to this day, whenever I hear 'Diana,' I remember my brother and me sitting in the music room as the long shadows of the late afternoon began to darken the room listening to the same song over and over again.

"I had planned to stay for about a week, but after a few days, my brother started to become really irritated about my presence and he started to yell at me. So the nurse told me that it would be better for him that I left sooner than later. When I last met him, he was in the wheelchair next to his bed with a cigarette hanging from his lips. The ashes were falling on his stomach. I tried to wipe it off and he began crying. I could not control myself, I started to cry too. I put my hand on his shoulders, and he cried as though the years of pain kept tightly wound up in his stomach were finally being released. He cried more like a wounded animal than a wounded soldier. I have never heard somebody cry like that before or after.

"My mother waited and waited for him to return. She would wait for the postman to come every day. You know how it rains in Hilo, but she would stand by the mailbox without any umbrella and look for the postman anxiously. He would say to her, 'Mrs. Arakawa, sorry, no mail today.' After a while, his letters stopped coming. I think she finally died from inexpressible sorrow. A mother's sadness for her child can never be adequately described with words."

My home in Hilo used to be walking distance to Momilani Cemetery near Kapiolani Street. The veterans cemetery is nearby. Sometimes when I would go to place flowers at the gravesites with my parents, I would look across the road and wonder what happened to Sergeant. ◆

KANSHA

One of the enduring memories of my maternal grandfather, Nihei Asano, is his early morning prayers. My mother's family lived in Mahaloa, a plantation camp surrounded by sugarcane fields consisting of sixteen or so families about two and a half miles from the town of Pāpaʻikou on Hawaiʻi Island. Because of its high elevation, it was cold during the winter months and whenever I visited my grandparents I would sleep under the thick *futon* (quilt blanket) my grandmother, Tome Asano, had made.

Both of my Asano grandparents had immigrated from Date Gun, Fukushima Ken (Prefecture), which is a region in the Snow Country in Japan. My grandfather did not talk much. He would sit on the *tatami* (straw matting) by the open window facing the sea, and he would ceremoniously take the Bull Durham tobacco from the bag and slowly tap the tobacco onto the tobacco wrapper, roll the wrapper, lick one end and strike the Swedish match to the rolled tobacco. With a gentle breeze blowing, the smoke would curl up to the open *tenjo* (ceiling) of the plantation house.

Whenever she had time, my grandmother would tell me how poor they had been in Fukushima and they had no alternative but to come to Hawaiʻi to seek a better life. She said that when it snowed, the snow would practically cover the house. She once mentioned that when she came to Mahaloa, there were no houses, and so, they had to live in grass huts like the native Hawaiians. When I first heard her description of her first home, I could not believe it until I saw a photograph of such a hut in a book celebrating the 100th anniversary of the beginning of Japanese immigration in Hawaiʻi.

My grandfather would wash his face and walk to the side entry of the house early in the morning just as the sun was peeking over the horizon. He would clap three times to let the Shinto gods know of his presence. Then he would express his thanks to the gods for all their blessings on every member of his family. He would thank the gods for their protection and their watchful eye on our health and safety. He would pray every morning until he was not physically able to do so, but even then he would pray from his bed.

As a young boy, there was something reassuring to me by my grand-father's early morning prayers of gratitude. He did not ask the gods for anything, nor did he plead for any special favors. He simply prayed in deep thanks. When I think about it now, my grandfather's prayers brought inner peace and spiritual comfort to everyone who could hear him in the early morning hours. After a while, I think everyone expected him to pray each morning. This communication between my grandfather and the gods was a special link, which we all appreciated.

With the experience of his harsh life, my grandfather's low mur-muring prayer of gratitude was sincere and deeply felt. When he prayed, I knew he was truly grateful.

When I visited my Asano grandparents, my grandmother would inevitably go to her garden, a plot of land in the community garden, to harvest whatever vegetables she had growing to have us take it home. She would harvest enough for her neighbors. She would say, "Shunji, *kinjo no shito ni yasai wo kubarimasho* (Let us distribute the vegetables to the neighbors)." I would ask why, and her response was, "*Minna no okagesame de seikatsu shitteimasu* (Because of everyone's kindness we live the life we do)." Implicit in her response was her recognition that everyone's cooperation, generosity and assistance made our lives more pleasant and bearable. No matter how difficult life may be, we must help each other and share whatever we have with others. We must be grateful when others share whatever they have with us.

My father who was ninety-three years old when he died would tell us about the kindness of others when he was growing up and he reminded us that we should be grateful for such kindness. One such act of kindness was extended to him by Yamauchi Sensei (teacher) and his wife. My father lived in Waiākea Camp 10, which is close to the forest line way above Hilo. Even today, it is a remote area of Hilo. Often times after a heavy rainfall, he would not be able to cross the stream to return home from school and would need to stay with Yamauchi

Sensei and his wife, who were Japanese language school teachers. My father would say, "Mrs. Yamaguchi was a very kind and understanding lady. She would give me plenty rice in the chawan because she knew it was hard for me to ask for a second bowl of rice. *Hontoni* nice lady *datta*. (She was a really nice lady). I always remember how nice she was to me." Mrs. Yamauchi's kindness was remembered and cherished for more than eighty-five years after by my father.

Often times I have heard that Japanese practice ancestor worship. I believe that prayers to our ancestors are not necessarily because we believe them to be deities. It may be more of a sense of gratitude for their deeds and to honor them. Without our ancestors, we would not be where we are today.

The issei deeply felt *kansha* (gratitude), because of their hardship and suffering. They truly appreciated whatever they had, because when they came to Hawai'i they had nothing but their hopes and other Meiji Era values. With their sense of gratitude, they never took anything for granted, however small or seemingly insignificant. Everyone and everything was to be appreciated.

I say Meiji Era values, because certain of the values that were instilled in us in Hawai'i were precepts taught and espoused during the Meiji Era. Some of the values are recognized in Japan, but they may be archaic in Japan today. Some of the Japanese think it is admirable that (Americans of Japanese ancestry) still practice these values.

One of the remembrances of my life's experiences is an elderly issei woman who offered incense at one of the special memorial services at 'Ōla'a Hongwanji in Kea'au on the Big Island when I was a young boy. She could barely walk to the front of the temple, but she did slowly and bowed low and reverently. She was neither self-conscious nor concerned about others in the temple waiting for their turn to offer incense. She clasped her hands in prayer and took a wisp of incense and placed it slowly into the incense bowl. She bowed deeply again and quietly said a prayer of thanksgiving. Her gratitude impressed me deeply and this scene has burned in my memory. This issei woman truly understood kansha.

Later nikkeijin generations have more material possessions. They attend prestigious schools and colleges, and have jobs their issei grandparents or great-grandparents would have difficulty understanding. The material progress made by the today's generation is evidence of the American Dream come true. However, the price the subsequent generations have paid for this progress is high, because they do not understand what it is to be truly grateful. What difference does it make to be truly grateful? When you are grateful, you appreciate what you have, how little it may be, and you are thankful for whatever condition your life may be at the moment. ◆

GIRL AT THE WINDOW

Before the 1960 tsunami a two-story building stood across the street from my father's hardware store on Kilauea Avenue. Now and then during the summer, Leilani, who used to live on the second floor, would wave at me from the open window of her apartment. She was pretty, pleasant and was always smiling. She looked like a poster girl for the Hawaiian tourism industry. She lived with an elderly woman and a younger brother. My good friend, Bert, told me, "Oh, yes, Leilani. She lives with her aunty."

In those days, early June to the end of August was a season of unhurried living, doing what we felt like doing each day as it came, without plans, without schedule and without having much to do. The protected world of my hometown was sheltered by a peaceful somnolence. The tranquility of those summers was not appreciated until they became a part of our memories. There are certain communities in the world where the vital sounds of the town are not trapped by a low hanging ceiling. All the sounds seem to rise and evaporate into the clouds. Such was the case for Hilo, where the quiet of the summer afternoons seem more pronounced, because no one and nothing was moving about. I still remember the brown mongrel dog snoozing in the shade of the barbershop and the Filipino barber napping on the tilted barber chair. It was as if God Himself was taking a siesta during those hot days of summer.

Leilani was younger than I, and we both attended Hilo High School. On campus, she would smile and say, "Hi, Roy. How are you?" Her smile was irresistible.

I would chat with her briefly. Her eyes always sparkled.

Bert once told me, "Do you know Leilani works at night as a waitress. A cocktail waitress. All the men adore her."

Some afternoons, I would see her brother talking to men. Then, he and the men would disappear for about an hour or so. Then, they would appear again from the back of the building. Sometimes, they were the same men. Sometimes not.

Before I left for college, I bumped into her at a nearby sundry store. She was by the magazine rack reading some Hollywood magazines.

I said, "Leilani, I won't see you for awhile. I'm going to a Mainland college. Take care of yourself."

Leilani replied, "Roy, thank you for being nice to me. I want to see you again. Don't get married to a Mainland girl."

I laughed and we parted. I didn't even hug her. I was sure I would see her again.

Years later Bert retuned to Hilo after working several years on the Mainland. He became the owner of an ice cream store near the mouth of Wailoa River in the same building where the fish auction is held. One day I went to his store and as I was eating my ice cream cone sitting on a bench outside he came out and we chatted about the old days.

I asked him, "Bert, whatever happened to Leilani? I don't see her anymore." By then, the 1960 tsunami had destroyed a large swath of Hilo town and the building where Leilani lived was gone.

Bert let out a heavy sigh. "Roy, did you know she had a tragic life. Her father killed her mother when she was young. Her father may still be in prison for the crime. That's why she had to live with her aunty near your father's store."

"I didn't know that. She was always smiling like she had no problems."

"Yeah, she was smiling on the outside but crying on the inside. I think she was very sad. After she graduated from high school, she continued to work as a waitress. The liquor inspectors knew she was not old enough to sell liquor at the restaurant, but they all looked away because they all knew about her sad life. One night one of the customers drove her home. The police think he was drunk. They got into an accident late at night. It was a one-car accident. He hit an electric pole. She died at the scene of the accident."

"Oh my god!"

"Do you know she had to work all the time because her aunty could not support Leilani and her brother? Young as she was, do you know she was a hooker even while she was in high school?"

"What! I can't believe it. She seemed so innocent."

Bert frowned, "I don't know why some people suffer so much when they are very nice and kind to other people." ◆

THE DUKE

He was an impressive looking man, much like an English lord in the movies. He carried himself in such a manly but casual manner that there was no question in my mind he was an aristocrat. He was tall, about six feet four or five inches, and weighed about 210 to 220 pounds. He had a ruddy face, his gray hair was swept back and he had a full mustache. When he walked, he strode with a gait of a military officer, someone born to command. It would not have surprised me, if he had been a general or a field marshal in the British army. He always seemed to have a pipe in his mouth, whether he smoked it or not I do not know. And, most unusual for Hawai'i at least, no matter what kind of weather it was, he wore a tweed coat, even on the hottest summer day.

I never learned his name or who he actually was. I don't know if he was gainfully employed at the time he lived in our town. How or where he got his money to live on, I don't think anyone really knew. He was certainly not a vagrant, because he seemed to have enough money to pay for whatever he purchased.

There was one thing he was known for. He could be seen walking far and wide, with a tan khaki cloth bag slung over his shoulder. No one really knew why he spent so much time just walking around. On one day, he could be seen walking in one part of town, and then, on another day, in another part of town. There was no apparent rhyme or reason where he walked.

He lived alone on the second floor of a rooming house near my father's hardware store. At night the light from a single electric bulb hanging from the ceiling, turned on and off with a chain, illuminated the somber room. Sometimes the police would be called when fights between inebriated tenants would get into a scuffle. I don't think he was the kind of person who would be a public nuisance. After all, he was an English gentleman.

I do not recall seeing him talk to anyone nor anyone to him. It could be that his regal appearance and military demeanor may have intimidated everyone.

One day, after a softball game as my friends and I sat under the old ironwood tree at Hilo Union School (my elementary school) facing the Catholic church, he walked by purposefully, looking straight ahead, like a swooping golden eagle, as he though he had an appointment to keep or a meeting to attend. I asked no one in particular, "I wonder who he is?"

"He sure is a mysterious guy. Just walks around all the time. I wonder why he does that?" asked Gary.

"You notice he always carries that bag with him. It doesn't seem to be filled with anything. It seems empty most of the time. Why carry a bag, if you don't have anything to carry?" asked Walter.

"I've never seen him smile, always so serious. He seems to have something on his mind, heavy in thought, smoking his pipe. Somehow, he gives me an impression that he lives in a world of his own, one that we don't exist, if you know what I mean," said Gary.

"I know something about him," said Nick. "My father learned about him when he worked as a police officer."

"Well, are you going to tell us, or is it some deep secret you're not free to share with us, eh, Nicky?" asked Walter.

Nick responded, "It's not a secret. My father told me he's an English-man, that he was an officer in World War I. He had a bad experience in one of the bloody battles in France or someplace like that, that he suffered shell shock. He might even be a lord or something like that."

"Yeah, maybe a duke, huh?" asked Gary.

"He sure looks like a duke," said Walter. "I wonder why he doesn't go back to England? You would think he would want to see his family. I know I would."

"It could be that he doesn't have any family back in England or anywhere, for that matter. Have you thought of that? After all, it's about thirty years since World War I ended," said Nick.

"He must be a lonely man," I said. "He lives alone, talks to no one and probably has no friends."

"He might still be so shell-shocked he doesn't know the difference," said Walter.

Months later, I saw him walking briskly past my father's store and as always he had his bag over his shoulder.

"Dad, have you ever wondered what he has in his bag?" I asked.

"No, never," my father answered. "What he has or doesn't have is strictly his business. I have enough to do without minding other people's business. This would be a better world if more people minded their own business."

"I know, but I'm still curious. I'd sure like to know what he has in his bag. He always carries it with him wherever he goes. It never seems to be full," I said.

"Roy, what is more important to me is that he doesn't have much in his bag. I admire him more for carrying an empty bag. I give him credit for doing that," my father responded.

"I don't understand what you mean?"

"Most people are burdened by their worldly possessions. We all have a desire to acquire things and to hoard what we acquire, and because we are afraid others may steal what we own we must carry what we own wherever we go. The more we acquire, the more baggage we must carry. What a heavy burden it becomes. The truly free man is someone who is not weighed down by all his possessions. As you say, the Englishman's bag is never full. It just might be that the less there is in his bag, the more content he is. I never see him look angry, or worried, or upset or annoyed. Have you?"

I had not.

"Do you notice he's always by himself. He must be lonely, huh, Dad?"

"Not necessarily. We think that someone is lonely because he is always alone. Who knows? He may prefer to be alone. Some people are surrounded by many people, and yet, they are very lonely."

My father was right on that point. We can be surrounded by a lot of people, but unless we have a meaningful relationship with those around us, we can still be awfully lonely. In fact, sometimes loneliness can be accentuated by the crowd around us, particularly if no one really cares for you one way or the other. Being a solitary person does not necessarily mean loneliness. Some may seek solitude for the peace and quiet it brings. Loneliness is a state of mind. It depends how you think and feel about your situation. If you seek it, the solitude is a long-sought luxury, and if you abhor it, it is misery.

"He never talks to anyone. Wouldn't you think he would be happier if he talked to people?"

"He could be, but then, he might not be. Some people talk, talk, talk. They talk a lot. They love to hear their own voice. They don't give others a chance to talk. After awhile, sadly for them, no one listens."

My father may have been right again. Even when two people talk to each other, unless one listens to the other, there is no communication. The words pass each other like wind in the forest, only sounds with no meaning. Others rant and rave. There is no dialogue. It is simply noise and after awhile everybody gets turned off because it becomes an annoyance and a nuisance. More people should remain silent. Then, when they speak, people will be more apt to listen to them.

"And, then, again, Roy, maybe the Englishman has nothing to say. Maybe he saw so much and experienced so much that he has gained wisdom. They say that a wise man doesn't talk too much."

My Kodani grandmother lived alone. Once when my father and I visited her, she said in her Hiroshima dialect, "Maybe I lived too long. It is amazing how fast time flies. I get up in the morning, cook my breakfast and eat alone. My lady friends come to visit me and we talk, and before I know it, another day is gone. I live alone, but I am not lonely for some reason. There are always things to do. I don't just sit and think. If I think, *hontoni arigatai* (truly grateful), *honma yo* (it really is)."

The Englishman bothered no one. He came and went as he pleased. He was like a pilgrim on a journey searching for something. Now and then I would see him standing under the shade of a tree with a pipe in his mouth. Who knows what he was thinking about? Maybe, he was not thinking at all. Could it be that he was happy simply walking around enjoying the scenery? He may have made peace with himself, and as a result, he had found serenity, unlike most of us. We are filled with turmoil, agitated and have inner conflicts. He knew his limitations. He was satisfied and most likely grateful for what he had. He was content with his life. What more could a person ask for? When you come down to it, there aren't too many people who are truly content with life as it is.

One day a group of us boys were hanging out in Mr. Higa's garage talking about a John Wayne movie we had just seen at the Mamo Theater. Mr. Higa was a 442nd Regimental Combat Team veteran. He was a close family friend who was good at fixing things. He had fought in Italy and France and had been wounded in the battle in France ordered by the Army higher-ups to save some Texan soldiers surrounded by the German Army. He now walked with a limp. The Japanese-American soldiers were dispensable. Their parents, spouses and relatives never complained to the politicians about where they fought and how they were used in battle. The term "cannon fodder" was never heard.

As Mr. Higa listened to us he shook his head. "Da real ting is not like da movies. I hope you boys nevah, nevah see da real ting. War is dirty business. It's da closest ting to hell in dis life. Da guys who really wen fight in battles no talk about war, because it brings back bad memories. Da only time I remema my war experience is wen I have nightmares, and I tell you, I still have nightmares, even after so many years. I get up sweating. Something triggers my war experience. What, I don't know. Da first time I was in battle, I was so scared, I shit in my pants...I no can change my pants. Da Germans shooting at us from high on top dis steep hill in Italy. Bazookas. Rockets. Shrapnel. Da goddamn howitzers. Machine guns. Da noise. Da yelling. Me, I'm surprised more guys don't die from fear. Den guys start dying around me...guys I knew. Dey don't show you in da movies, but in real war, men get blown to bits. Heads get blasted off. Hands and legs come off. Guts pour out from da stomach. Guys try to help, but many guys are shocked. Da guys cry when de see da friends all shot to hell. Guys yell out, 'Okasan! Okasan!'

"Wen dey yell out for da mama like dat, you know dey no more chance. I nevah could figure out why dey call out for their mama like dat. Flies on da dead bodies. Da smell of shot up bodies. You see all kinds of guys in battle. Da true self comes out. Da guys who brag cannot move. Da small, quiet guys become real heroes. Sometimes, sergeants practically take over from da captains and lead da men on. In da summer, it's hot and stink. Our feet get toe jams. In da winta, it's so frigging cold, you can hardly move, especially us guys from Hawai'i...we're not used to cold and da snow and da ice on da ground. We want to rest, but headquarters order us to move to da front. Cannot argue. Just obey. Sometimes I know some of us gonna die, and sure ting, guarantee, guys die. Some get shot up really bad. All bust up. In bad pain for years and years. Dey end up in military hospitals. Dey nevah come home."

One late Saturday afternoon, about closing time at the store, I hear my mother talking to someone. I looked out to see who it was. Holy Bejesus! I couldn't believe it. My mother was talking to the Duke. I sauntered over to listen.

My mother was saying, "The days are getting short so you should be careful when you are walking in the late afternoon, sometimes people in their cars cannot see people walking along the road."

"Thank you. I do appreciate your concern," the Duke responded. He sort of saluted my mother and put his pipe back in his mouth and strode toward his rooming house.

"Ma, I didn't know you talked to the Englishman," I said.

"I smile and say hello to him or to anyone that pass by, Roy. If you want people to be friendly, you have to be nice to them. The Englishman is gentleman. Ever since I've started to say hello, he stops and asks me how I am. He talks about the plants we sell and he tells me about the plants he sees while he is walking around."

"Ma, I'm surprised he talks to you. I've never seen him talk to anyone."

"Sometimes you have to say something first before the other person will talk to you, Roy. You'll never know if someone is friendly or not, unless you extend your welcome hand first. It's as simple as that."

As the sun set one late October day, I looked up and saw the Duke sitting on a high-back rattan chair, looking out toward the sea. He just sat there, looking out. The sounds of the day faded into the quiet of a still Hilo night. If, as Mr. Higa said, he didn't like to think about war, and if the Duke didn't return to England because he wished to be as far away from home as possible, I wondered what the Duke was thinking about hour after hour, staring at the distant horizon. Hilo then had no television. Did he listen to the radio? Did he read a book? Did he go to the movies? As the curtain of night descended, there was only darkness. Nothing could be seen in Hilo Bay, but the Duke continued to sit there, looking out toward the distant horizon. ♦

ACKNOWLEDGMENTS

My appreciation to Allisha Furuya and Hiroko Matsubara for their hard work, diligence and valuable time in making this book a reality. I also wish to express my thanks to George Engebretson of Watermark Publishing for his patience and assistance.

ABOUT THE AUTHOR

Roy Kodani was born, raised and educated in Hilo, Hawai'i. He grew up on the Big Island—when sugar was king and the plantation system shaped the fabric of society—and graduated from Hilo High School, where he learned English grammar in, ironically, his Latin class.

Kodani's first publication was an essay written in the seventh grade for the Hilo Intermediate School literary magazine. The experience motivated him to continue writing. "To see your writing in print is a marvelous experience," he says. He graduated from Lafayette College in Easton, Pennsylvania, where he was further influenced by the school's talented and capable professors of English and literature. Thereafter, he graduated from the George Washington University Law School in Washington, D.C. and upon his return to the Islands was hired as a deputy attorney general for the State of Hawai'i.

Kodani currently practices law as an international attorney in Asia, traveling to Japan, China, Korea and Mongolia. As a public service to his local community, he also offers his services to nonprofit organizations and churches. Kodani paints with oils, swims, plays racquetball, travels, lectures and continues to write.

Made in the USA
Monee, IL
14 October 2020

45054318R00115